Land of Our Lady Series

Hymns to Mary

HISTORY OF HYMNS. A hymn is a song of praise to God or the Blessed Mother or the Saints. Hymns date back to very ancient times. Pagan people sang hymns to their gods and heroes. The earliest hymn we know about was sung by the Babylonians. This hymn tells about the creation of the world. The Jews sang hymns in praise of the true God. These hymns are called psalms. The Bible tells us that the night before Jesus died the Apostles sang a hymn at the Last Supper.

ORIGIN AND MEANING. "Hail, Holy Queen, Enthroned Above" is like the "Salve Regina." The "Salve Regina" ("Hail, Holy Queen") was ordered to be said after every low Mass. We can take "Hail Holy Queen, Enthroned Above," line by line and match it with the "Salve Regina." We find that they are almost the same. It is among the prayers said for the conversion of Russia. We do not know the author of "Hail, Holy Queen, Enthroned Above." Whoever he was, he must have loved Our Lady very much.

Hail, Holy Queen Enthroned Above

Hail, Holy Queen Enthroned Above, O Maria.
Hail, Mother of Mercy and of love, O Maria.

REFRAIN

Triumph all ye Cherubim,
Sing with us, ye Seraphim;
Heaven and earth resound the hymn,
Salve, Salve, Salve Regina.

Our Life, our sweetness here below, O Maria.
Our hope in sorrow and in woe, O Maria.

REFRAIN

To thee we cry poor sons of Eve, O Maria.
To thee we sigh, we mourn, we grieve, O Maria.

REFRAIN

This earth is but a vale of tears, O Maria.
A place of banishment and fears, O Maria.

REFRAIN

Turn then most gracious advocate, O Maria.
Towards us thine eyes compassionate, O Maria.

REFRAIN

When our exile is complete, O Maria.
Show us thy Son, our Jesus sweet, O Maria.

REFRAIN

O clement, O gracious, Mother sweet, O Maria.
O Virgin Mary we entreat, O Maria.

REFRAIN

APPLICATION. Mary is the Mother of Mercy.
How comforting it is to know that in discouragement and loneliness you always go to your mother, and through prayer you seek the mercy of Mary.

Courtesy of Rev. J. B. Carol, O. F. M.

Land of Our Lady Series

Founders
of
Freedom

by Sister M. Benedict Joseph, S.N.J.M.

EDITOR-IN-CHIEF:
Rev. Timothy F. O'Leary, Ph.D.
Assistant Superintendent of Schools
Archdiocese of Boston

ASSISTANT EDITOR-IN-CHIEF:
Sister M. Veronica, S.P.B.V.

CO-EDITORS:
Rt. Rev. Clarence E. Elwell, Ph.D.
Superintendent of Schools
Diocese of Cleveland

Rev. Patrick J. Roche, Ph.D.
Assistant Superintendent of Schools
Archdiocese of Los Angeles

Neumann Press
Charlotte, North Carolina

Land of Our Lady Series—Book One
Founders of Freedom

Published by Neumann Press, an imprint of TAN Books. Originally published as: "Land of Our Lady Series"—Founders of Freedom, Benziger Brothers, Inc., 1954. Revised edition with color corrections, cover design copyright © Neumann Press.

ISBN: 978-0-911845-53-2

Printed and bound in the United States of America.

Neumann Press
Charlotte, North Carolina
www.NeumannPress.com

2014

EDITORS' INTRODUCTION

A heritage whose value is not appreciated is a heritage in danger of being lost. For citizens who fail to realize that freedom is their most precious natural gift may easily surrender it, either to the tyrant who offers them a choice between liberty and death, or to the State which promises them the spurious security of faceless men. With the loss of freedom, whether snatched away by the hand of the despot or worn away by the slow erosion of an inhuman social climate, there vanishes that priceless personal dignity which distinguishes man as man. To be preserved, freedom must be cherished. Hence the importance of this History Series, through whose pages is woven, like a golden thread, the Christian tradition of human freedom.

We cannot cherish something which we do not understand. Emotional aspirations, sentimental attachment, unflinching allegiance of heart and will, cannot be sustained unless these driving forces be rooted in concepts which are valid and enduring. It is true that our age speaks much of freedom. But to talk of freedom is not enough; we must know what freedom is. To some, the word freedom is synonymous with caprice; to others, it connotes a vagrant sense of irresponsibility. In either usage, the concept of freedom is a negative one; freedom is judged to be an end in itself, apart from orientation to any purpose or goal, divorced from any consideration of the end of human existence. In such a framework of thought, the free man has no more dignity than the scudding cloud driven across the sky by the strength of the prevailing wind, or the tumbleweed pursuing its erratic course across the prairies at the mercy of the forces of nature which spawned it. The Christian concept of freedom is rooted in the Christian concept of man as a being whose end reaches into infinity, with a destiny beyond himself, and a final goal wrapped in the possession of the God Who made him. Because man has this sublime purpose in his existence, then is freedom precious, because it enables man to find release from those forces which would impede his progress towards his God.

The present volume seeks to sketch in broad outline the story of freedom's birth in the creative mind of God, the original transmission of this gift to man, its impairment through the human tragedy of sin, and the halting steps taken in the long centuries of Pre-Christian History to restore it once again. With the coming of Christ, a new era in human freedom dawned. Restored to the dignity of sons of God, men awoke to that freedom with which God had made them free. The passing centuries saw that freedom grow and expand in the climate of

7

Christian civilization, so that today we are the heirs of a legacy which ripened in the Western world. If we are the heirs, we are the custodians also; freedom is a victory which must be won and re-won in every century, and indeed, in the kingdom of each man's soul.

The tragic error of ancient Esau has become proverbial, in that he sold his birthright for a mess of pottage. It is the hope of the editors that our youth, learning the bright history of freedom in this Series, will cherish their birthright and will yield it to no other prize.

THE EDITORS.

CONTENTS

UNIT ONE

CIVILIZATION BEGINS

UNIT TWO

CIVILIZATION DEVELOPS

UNIT THREE

CIVILIZATION IS CHRISTIANIZED

UNIT FOUR

CHRISTIAN CIVILIZATION IS CHALLENGED

UNIT FIVE

THE CHURCH SAVES CHRISTIAN CIVILIZATION

FOREWORD

THE publication of the "Land of Our Lady" Series marks a notable advancement in the field of history textbooks for Catholic elementary schools. The Series fulfills very effectively the need for history textbooks that are devoid of secularistic and materialistic tendencies and based on the sound principles of Christianity and therefore, a Christian philosophy of history.

This Series includes not only the factual data that comprise the history of America as a nation, but it incorporates also those elements of American Catholic history that can be assimilated by pupils of the elementary school level. The growth and development of the Catholic Church in the United States parallels the content of American history in each textbook of the Series.

The greatest contribution of these texts to the training and schooling of young American Catholic boys and girls is the manner in which Christian social principles are woven in the texts. As the various events of history are taken up for study, the textbooks point out the positive or negative correlation of the factual data to the principles of Christian social living.

We are grateful to the firm of Benziger Brothers, and to the competent Board of Editors and Authors for the task they have successfully accomplished in producing this American Catholic Series, "Land of Our Lady."

RT. REV. FREDERICK G. HOCHWALT, PH.D.
SECRETARY GENERAL, N.C.E.A.

Hymns to Mary

HISTORY OF HYMNS. Some of the earliest hymns of the Catholic Church were in Greek. One of these early Greek hymns, "O Gladsome Light," has been translated by the American poet, Longfellow. It is found in his book, "The Golden Legend." In the eastern part of the Roman Empire the heretics used hymns to spread their false teachings. St. Ephrem (307–373) wrote Catholic hymns to defeat the work of the heretics.

ORIGIN AND MEANING. In 1858 the Blessed Virgin appeared to a fourteen year old girl, Bernadette, at Lourdes, France. Mary, "the beautiful Lady," said, "I am the Immaculate Conception." She told Bernadette that a church was to be built there and that processions should be made to this church. Mary also caused a spring to flow. She promised to help those who bathed there. Today many people make processions to this spot. They pray that Mary will help them. At the evening processions all carry torches and sing the hymn, "Immaculate Mary."

Immaculate Mary

Immaculate Mary!
Our hearts are on fire;
That title so wondrous
Fills all our desire!
Ave, Ave, Ave, Maria!
Ave, Ave, Maria!

We pray for our Mother,
The church upon earth,
And bless, sweetest Lady,
The land of our birth,
Ave, Ave, Ave, Maria!
Ave, Ave, Maria!

We pray for God's glory,
May His Kingdom come;
We pray for His Vicar
Our Father in Rome.
Ave, Ave, Ave, Maria!
Ave, Ave, Maria!

O Mary! O Mother!
Reign o'er us once more:
Be all lands thy dowry,
As in days of yore.
Ave, Ave, Ave, Maria!
Ave, Ave, Maria!

APPLICATION. Mary is Immaculate, living a life that is all pure and without sin.
As we choose friends and companions, we also pattern our lives on the good points we see in others. The thoughts and ideals which we picture for ourselves are exemplified by the life of Mary.

Courtesy of Rev. J. B. Carol, O. F. M.

UNIT ONE

CIVILIZATION BEGINS

CHAPTER I—CREATION OF ADAM AND EVE
Gifts of God to Mankind
Results of Sin
Adam's Children Forget God
The Ark and the Flood
The Tower of Babel

CHAPTER II—CIVILIZATION GROWS IN OTHER LANDS
Some Useful Inventions Made by Early Man
Chinese Beginnings of Civilization
Gifts from Egypt
Babylonian Teachers of Law and Science
Phoenician Carriers of Civilization

CHAPTER III—GOD'S PROMISES KEPT ALIVE BY THE HEBREWS
Teachers of the True Religion
Abraham—Father of the Chosen People
Punishment of the Israelites
God Gives the Commandments through Moses
Israelites in the Promised Land

UNIT ONE

CIVILIZATION BEGINS

THIS year we shall study some important history stories. Some of these stories will take us back to the beginning of the world. We shall learn about some of the wonderful things that happened a very long time ago.

The part of the world we live in is called America. But it did not always look the way it does today. There was once a time when no white men lived here. There was once a time when no one in Europe knew anything about America. Then Columbus discovered America in 1492. Soon people began to call this newly-found land the "New World." When people talk about the other places on earth, they call those lands the "Old World." The stories in this book are really the history of the Old World.

In this Unit you will learn about the unhappy results of the sin of our first parents. You will study about the gifts that the Chinese gave to civilization in the early times. Then you will read about the Egyptians. You will discover that you owe them much for their gifts to the world. The Babylonians were another early people. You will find many interesting things about them.

The story of the Phoenicians will always be remembered. It is a story of sailors, fishermen, and traders.

The greatest gifts of all came from the Hebrew people. They gave us the knowledge of the true God and kept alive the promise of a Redeemer. They were the Chosen People of God.

CHAPTER I

CREATION OF ADAM AND EVE

A glance at the chapter. You have learned from your catechism that God had no beginning and will have no end. Because He is completely happy and good He wanted to share His happiness and goodness. That is why He decided to create man and all the beautiful things in the world for man to use.

You have learned from your Bible History that God created the first man and woman. We call Adam the father of all mankind. He is the head of the great family of human beings. You and I, and every person in the world, belong to this large family. It makes no difference whether our skin is black, white, red, or yellow. We are all children of Adam and Eve.

When God made the world, He put everything in order. When Adam sinned, he destroyed the order that God had made. He lost many gifts also.

Sin always brings unhappiness.

In this chapter you will learn how Adam's children kept or broke God's Laws. You will see how early men searched for the happiness lost by sin. They moved to other lands. Soon new ways of living began. This was the beginning of civilization.

1. Gifts of God to Mankind

Besides giving life to man, God gave man even greater gifts. He made him to His own image and likeness. He gave man understanding and free will. These gifts were not given to any other creature on earth. That is why man is higher than any of the other living things on earth.

All men in one family. You know that Adam is the father of all men on earth. All men on earth are brothers in the same family. All are equal before God and men. The earth was made for man. Each of us must use it for

God's glory. No man should hate any other man. No race and no people may claim the goods of the earth for itself alone.

A share in divine life. God filled the souls of Adam and Eve with sanctifying grace. This means that God gave them a share in His own divine life. He promised that they would live forever if they would love and obey Him. God gave Adam and Eve a beautiful place on this earth to live in. It was called Paradise.

Adam and Eve had free will. They could obey God or disobey Him, if they chose to do so. To test their love and obedience, God asked them not to eat the fruit of one tree. He told them they would have to suffer and die if they ate it.

2. Results of Sin

Your Bible History has told you the sad story of the fall of our first parents. You know that Eve listened to the devil and ate some of the forbidden fruit. She gave some to Adam. The devil promised that they could become like God if they ate this fruit.

Disobedience is a sin. This first sin was very serious because Adam and Eve knew very well they were doing wrong. This sin of pride made them disobey God. It put God's plan for the world out of order. It made Adam and Eve lose the friendship of Almighty God.

God's plans were upset by this sin of Adam. Adam's sin did something to us. We call what it did to us *original sin.*

Paradise lost to Adam and Eve. When Adam and Eve saw what they had done they were afraid. They tried to hide from God. God called them and told them they would have to leave Paradise. He said they would have to work hard for their food and would suffer pain, sorrow, and death. Now it would be hard for them to be good because they had committed sin.

As you know, we are all children of Adam. If he had been obedient to God's wishes, we would have shared all his happiness. But all of us must share in his punishment because he sinned against his loving God. We, too, have to work hard, to suffer pain, sorrow, and death. Because we are children of Adam, the devil tries to make us commit sin also.

God's promise. Although God drove Adam and Eve out of the garden of Paradise, He was sorry for them. He promised them a Redeemer. The Redeemer would make up for what they had lost by their sin and would do much more for us.

Who would win back for us the gifts lost by sin? Only God could win them back because man had offended God and could never make up to God for his sin.

The Son of God, the Second Person of the Holy Trinity, would come to earth. He would be a man like us, through Mary, His Holy Mother. Eve, a woman, led man into sin. Mary, a woman who would be God's Mother, would offer her Son to redeem man from sin.

3. Adam's Children Forget God

Cain and Abel. Our first parents had many children, the first of whom were Cain and Abel. These children were taught to offer sacrifices to God. Abel pleased God with his sacrifices. Cain made God angry because he was selfish. Cain became jealous of his brother and killed him.

Jealousy and hate make men do terrible things. They cause unhappiness in families and wars in the world.

Evil begins. Soon the human family became very large. The names of all Adam's children are not given in the Bible. We know from the Bible, however, that Seth was one of Adam's children. He was very good and taught his children to love God and to obey His laws. Seth's children were called the *children of God*. The children of Cain were wicked and were called *children of men*. They were called by this name because they did not obey God's laws. They thought only of themselves.

While the children of Seth served God they were happy. When some of them married the sons and daughters of Cain they, too, soon became wicked. After a while the world became a very evil place. People became unhappy because they were no longer God's friends.

4. The Ark and the Flood

Although it was very hard to be good when there was so much evil around, one man and his family did remain good. He was Noe. The name Noe means "rest" or "comfort." From his family in years to come the Redeemer would be born.

The spread of evil. The human family was growing larger and larger. New cities were growing up. Many people in these cities were evil. They did not pray to God nor keep God's laws.

God was very angry with man and decided to send a flood to destroy the things He had created. God willed to save Noe and his family. You know how He told Noe to make an ark which would float on the waters. It would protect those who were in it. Noe and his sons built the ark exactly as God told them.

Finally it was finished. God told Noe to take animals of every kind into the ark. Noe and his family went into the ark. Then God sent the flood. Soon the waters had covered the highest mountain. All living things in that part of the world were destroyed.

Some time later God told Noe to take his family and all living creatures out of the ark and settle on the earth. He commanded them to increase and multiply. Noe offered sacrifice to adore, thank, and praise God. He begged God's pardon and blessing. Then God promised that He would never destroy

The ark comes to rest after the flood

Culver Service

The tower of Babel

Sem and his children settled in Asia.

As these people moved from country to country, they were always looking for happiness. They always kept in mind the promise of a Redeemer which God had made to Adam. They invented many things. They found many different kinds of food. But still they were unhappy and restless. They always wanted something more or something different.

5. The Tower of Babel

the earth by flood again. As a sign of His promise He placed a rainbow in the sky.

God commanded Noe's family to increase and multiply and fill the earth. Because of this command, Noe has been called *the second father of the human race.*

The sons of Noe. The sons of Noe were Sem, Cham (kam), and Japheth (jay'-feth). These sons had many children. Cham and his family lived in Syria and Africa. The children of Japheth spread about Europe.

Another sin of pride. Some of these people did not believe God when He said He would never send another flood to destroy the earth. They began to build a tower to reach the sky. They hoped to make a great name for themselves. God was displeased because they were so proud. God allowed them to quarrel among themselves. Soon everything became confused. The place where this happened is called *Babylon* or "place of confusion." When men do not trust God they cannot work together.

Word Study

civilization	knowledge	sanctifying	sacrifice	human
jealousy	increase	multiply	confusion	
displeased	Babylon	invented	restless	

20

To Help You Understand

1. Ask your teacher to show you the difference between sizes of the Old World and the New World. Find the Eastern Hemisphere and the Western Hemisphere on your globe or wall map. Which of these is called the Old World?

2. Find a map in your geography book that contains the Eastern Hemisphere. Reread the preview of this Unit to find out why you are going to study about the Old World this year.

3. Collect pictures of different kinds of people, such as Indians, Negroes, Whites, Filipinos, Chinese, etc. Paste them together to make one large picture. Over the picture write the words: "We are all members of the same human family. Our parents are Adam and Eve." You might find the pictures you need in your Holy Childhood magazine or other missionary magazines or in newspapers.

Work by Yourself

Can you work by yourself? This exercise will prove to your teacher if you can do so. Number your paper 1 to 7. After each number write the page of your textbook on which you found the answer to these questions.

1. From whom do we receive very great gifts?

2. Where did the New World receive its first idea of freedom?

3. What is another word for "way of living"?

4. What does sin always bring to people?

5. Who is called the second father of the human race? Why?

6. Why should we love all men as brothers?

7. What is the work of a Redeemer, and who can act as a Redeemer?

For a Higher Mark

If you can talk over these questions with your classmates, your teacher will give you some extra points towards your history mark in her record book.

1. How can we show in our daily lives that we believe that all men are made to the image and likeness of God?

2. Why were the children of Cain called "children of men"?

3. Why was there confusion after people started to build the Tower of Babel?

4. Why is there so much unhappiness in families and wars in the world?

5. Why is this history book called "Founders of Freedom"?

CHAPTER II

CIVILIZATION GROWS IN OTHER LANDS

A look into the past. Can you think of a time when no one knew how to write? This fact was really true a long time ago. The first kind of writing was made by drawing pictures. These pictures told stories.

Later, signs were made to stand for certain words. Afterwards, people began to use letters of the alphabet for writing. Which of these kinds of writing do we use today?

This chapter tells how civilization grew among early peoples. It tells not only about the early kinds of writing, but also the most important things that these early peoples gave to civilization.

1. Some Useful Inventions Made by Early Man

Man discovers new things. In the early days people could not write. Because of this, no his-

tory of the very early period was written.

We call this very early period by a long name. We can build up this word ourselves. Write the word "historic" on your paper. Now place in front of this word the letters "pre." These three letters mean "before." So *Prehistoric Age* means the period before history was written.

The Prehistoric Age is divided into three periods or steps of progress. These are called the *Old Stone Age,* the *New Stone Age,* and the *Age of Metals.* We know about this early period because we have found tools and drawings left behind by early man.

After Adam's fall, man's mind was slower to learn than Adam's had been. Before man learned to live in houses, he lived in caves. Little by little,

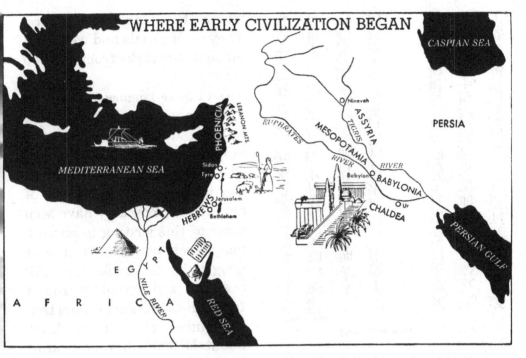

WHERE EARLY CIVILIZATION BEGAN

however, he began to make use of stone and metal for tools and weapons. Man learned how to use plants and animals for food and clothing. He took milk from the cow and the goat and made butter and cheese.

Later man discovered that he could get a spark of fire by rubbing two sticks together. He used to build his fire on a flat stone at the opening of his cave. Can you tell why he built his fire at that place?

Fire not only protected man from wild beasts. He used fire to prepare his food and to keep him warm. Fire also helped him to shape metal tools and arms. **Man's search for happiness.** In

the beginning, man had no way of writing the words he used in speaking to others. He did not say or use numbers like ours. He had a strange way of counting, saying "as many as the eyes, the fingers, or the toes."

Because of Adam's fall, it was hard for people to learn. Man kept seeking happiness. He tried to find it in many ways. He wandered from place to place, using the gifts of the earth and inventing things for his use. He did not seem to understand that happiness consists in serving God.

2. Chinese Beginnings of Civilization

China in early days. China is

Chinese writing

probably the oldest highly civilized nation. We do not find a record of all the Chinese did. We know, however, many things the Chinese did before other nations.

When Europe was just beginning to grow civilized, the Chinese had already used movable type to print books. They painted beautiful landscapes. Their farmers tilled the soil with a stone-bladed hoe.

Leaders in inventions. The early Chinese must have been a very inventive people. They were the first to use a compass for finding directions.

The Chinese were also the first to use gunpowder from which they made firecrackers. They built canals and wells and made waterworks from bamboo cane.

The Chinese language. The Chinese language is very difficult to learn. It is the oldest written language we have in the world. The Chinese language does not use letters. It is a system of characters. You may have seen some of this writing in mission magazines, or perhaps in your geography textbook. The Chinese use a different character for each word. This means that a Chinese child must learn about 50,000 different characters. How many letters are in our alphabet? The Chinese do not read across the page as we do. They read and write from top to bottom of the page instead.

The Great Wall of China. Warlike people often came to China. They tried to take away the land that belonged to the Chinese. Emperor Chin united the states of China under one government.

To keep out enemies Emperor Chin began to build a great wall around China. It forms the northern border of the country and is 1500 miles long. This "Great Wall of China" took ten years for thousands of workers to build it. It is the greatest wall any country ever built to protect itself.

A great Chinese teacher. About five hundred years before Christ was born, there lived in China a great teacher. His name was Confucius (kon-few'-shus). This man taught his pupils to live a good life by following the laws which God has placed in the mind of man.

One of Confucius' most important teachings was respect for parents. With the Chinese, love for the family must come first. They carried this respect too far. They worshipped their dead parents and grandparents as if they were gods. This is called ancestor worship. Can you tell from this the meaning of ancestor? Do you honor your dead ancestors?

This false worship has kept many of the Chinese from learning about the one True God. It has kept them from making other progress in learning.

Golden sayings of Confucius. Confucius did not try to establish a religion. He taught his pupils more about government than about God or about life after death. He said many wise things that have come down to us as proverbs, such as: "What you do not wish done to yourself, do not do to others."

Confucius thought that men could live good lives just by following the example of other good men. He taught that the first duty of friends is to help one another. But we must remember that we must help our enemies too. That is the kind of goodness Christ taught.

Chinese children had schools long before the children of other nations. In their schools the Chinese learned about Confucius, the great Chinese teacher.

3. Gifts from Egypt

You already know from the Bible that Noe had three sons. One of these was Cham. Cham's grandchildren wandered from place to place looking for water and grazing land for their flocks.

Finally they came upon the Nile River, which is in Egypt. At certain times in the year the Nile River would overflow. It would spread over a vast area of land on both sides of the river. When the waters went down rich mud was left. Much grain and wheat could be grown on this rich soil. Because of this, Egypt is called the Gift of the Nile.

The Great Wall of China extends for many miles

Egyptian farmers. Although the Nile Valley was excellent farm land, the methods of farming were very poor. Crude plows were drawn by oxen, and the farmers scattered the seeds by hand.

However, the Egyptians knew how to catch the river water by digging holes in the ground. These large holes were used to store the water until the dry season. Then the farmers would direct this water to their crops by means of ditches. In this way their crops received the necessary water. We say that the Egyptians knew how to irrigate their crops. This was the first successful means of *irrigation*. It enabled the Egyptians to grow plenty of food for themselves and for their neighbors.

The growth of Egypt. Egypt became a vast empire with many beautiful palaces and temples in its cities. The principal city was Thebes (theebz). The Egyptians worshipped many gods and each city had its own god. Because the sun seemed to give life to plants, animals, and man, it was believed to be god.

26

Egypt ruled by Pharaos. The Pharao (fair'-owe) was the ruler of all the people. The name Pharao means "great house." He was called by this name because he lived in a large palace and had a large court. The priests of the temple and soldiers helped him make the laws and carry on the government.

The people paid taxes by giving the government farm products, cattle, and labor. Many of the Pharaos were cruel. They taxed the people too much and made them work hard on public buildings. If the people refused, they were severely punished. The Pharaos, when they died, had themselves buried in huge pyramids. Within these pyramids were placed valuables which they thought would be necessary for them in the next world.

What made Egypt rich and famous. At times other countries suffered famines when plant and animal life was destroyed. To prevent starvation people would travel to Egypt to buy grain and supplies. This trade made the Egyptian empire rich and famous. In Egypt

The Sphinx, with pyramids in the background

the traders learned many things that were unknown in their own countries. Can you recall the story in your Bible History of a famous Hebrew family that came to Egypt to buy food?

Egyptian stone work. The Egyptians were great builders. They made slaves of those whom they had captured in war. These slaves had to carry heavy stones long distances and build high buildings.

Besides the palaces and temples, the Egyptians built large pyramids (pir′-a-mids). These were tombs or burial places. The Egyptians believed in life after death so they preserved the bodies of their dead with oils, gums, and spices. Then they wrapped them carefully in linen cloth. These preserved bodies are called *mummies.* Some have been found that are still well preserved. Food, clothing, and jewelry were also put into the tomb with the mummy. The Egyptians did this because they thought that dead persons would need these things in the life after death. Were the Egyptians right about the life after death?

Egyptians also built sphinxes (sfingk′-sez). A sphinx had the head of a human being and the

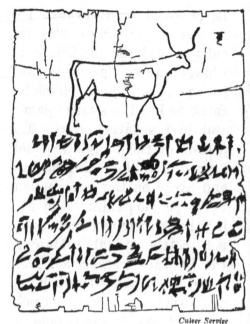

Egyptian writing

body of a lion. It was placed near a temple or tomb as a protection against harm. The Egyptians also made obelisks (ob′-e-lisks) in honor of the Sun-god. An obelisk is a tall, four-sided pillar that becomes smaller at the top. It was made from a single piece of stone.

The Egyptians start to write. The writing of the Egyptians was really pictures. These pictures are called hieroglyphics (higher-owe-glif′-iks). Later the Egyptians made up a more simplified form of writing. Much that we know about the Egyptians we have learned from their own writings in hieroglyphics.

For a long time no one knew how to read the Egyptian hieroglyphics.

In the year 1799, some French soldiers of Napoleon were preparing for a battle. While working in the city of Rosetta, at the mouth of the Nile River, they found a large stone slab with three kinds of writing on it. One kind was in the Greek language. Another was hieroglyphics. The third was in the simplified form of Egyptian writing.

Many people could read the Greek writing. They guessed that the same message was contained in the other two writings also. But no one could read them. After a long time had passed, a French scholar announced that he could read the Egyptian writings also.

This famous stone slab is called the *Rosetta Stone*. Because the stone gave the key to Egyptian writing, we know a great deal about the way the Egyptians lived and worked. We know what they believed to be the true religion.

The making of paper. Do you know where the word "paper" comes from? It comes from the name of a plant which grew along the banks of the Nile River. The plant was called *papyrus* (pa-pie´-rus). The Egyptians used to split a reed or stem of this plant and press it flat. This formed a kind of white paper. Their ink was made from a mixture of gum, black soot, and water. They used a sharp-pointed reed for a pen.

Other gifts from the Egyptians. Many writings on papyrus have been found in the pyramids. These tell us some of the things men thought about in the early days. They tell us some of the things these early people knew about surgery, medicine, and arithmetic.

We know from these writings on papyrus that the Egyptians studied the sun and the stars. Their study of the stars told them that a year had 365 days. The first day of the Nile flood was their New Year's Day. They surveyed their land, and each person's part was marked out exactly.

Egypt had developed the first great empire of civilization. For many centuries it was very successful. But its leaders became harsh and cruel. After some time it grew weak and failed. It was conquered by people known as Babylonians. However, we are grateful to the Egyptians for their gifts to our civilization.

Two big Egyptian obelisks

4. Babylonian Teachers of Law and Science

The land between two rivers. Another people of early times lived in a land east of Egypt, but north of the Arabian Desert. These people were nomads or wanderers. They owned large flocks of sheep and had to keep looking for new fields.

Some of these wandering shepherds found a rich valley that was not owned by anyone. They brought their sheep to this spot. Each leader claimed a share of the land. This land is a broad and fertile plain called Babylonia (bab-i-loe'-ni-a). It lies between two rivers, called the *Tigris* (tie'-gris) and *Euphrates* (you-fray'-teez). Do you know what this land is called today?

We shall read more about the people of this land. We shall see how their fertile homeland helped them to become strong and powerful. Soon they became one of the richest of peoples.

Shepherds become farmers. The soil of this place had been made rich or fertile by the overflow of the Tigris and the Euphrates Rivers. Many different kinds of plants could grow on this soil. This made the shepherds change their way of living. They became farmers. They built homes out of baked brick. They plowed the ground. They built canals so that they could bring water from the rivers to their crops and animals. These canals were also used for travel. When traveling on land, the Babylonians used an invention of their own. It was a cart with wheels.

Ruler of the Babylonians. The people did not have good leaders and were often unhappy. One tribe would envy another and make war. At last, the tribes found a great leader in Hammurabi (ham-oo-rah'-be). Even though he was a great soldier it took him thirty years to stop the warfare among the tribes. Then he had himself crowned king.

Hammurabi was a good ruler. Under his leadership Babylonia became rich, powerful, and famous. He made Babylon his chief city. Men from other countries brought their wares to Babylon. They brought such things as grain, dates, leather,

This is what Babylon looks like today

and wool. They traded these things with the Babylonians for clothes, copper, bronze, and other useful articles.

Laws of Hammurabi. Hammurabi collected all the old laws and customs of his people. When these laws had been put in order, he had them carved on a large flat piece of stone. This is the earliest list of laws that was put in writing. This *code,* or collection of laws, was the most important thing that Hammurabi gave to the world. This collection is called the *Code of Hammurabi.*

Some of Hammurabi's best laws were those that mentioned how women should be treated. Women were often looked upon as slaves in ancient times. Hammurabi's laws demanded that women should be treated with honor, respect, and protection.

Hammurabi was noted for being just, but his justice had very little forgiveness in it. Along with other pagans, he believed in harsh and cruel punishment for one's enemies. We know that Our Lord taught us to forgive those who harm us. This is God's rule. The pagans did not know all of God's rules.

Hammurabi also built schools to teach all the new things that men had learned from one another. In this way he saved what men had learned from being lost.

Babylonian writing. The Babylonians had a very difficult kind of writing. It was made up of many signs. These signs had to be combined to make a word. Each of these signs was shaped like a wedge. This writing was called *cuneiform* (kyou-nee'-i-form) or wedge-form writing. The writing was done on clay tablets which were later baked in the sun. Explorers since that time have found whole libraries of these clay books in Babylonia.

Some gifts of the Babylonians. These people had a knowledge of many things about government, laws, religion, and art. They kept written records of things they did. They also wrote bills for the goods they exchanged with their customers.

The Babylonians divided the year into months, weeks, and days. The new month always began with the new moon. From this we learn they studied *astronomy,* or the science of the heavenly bodies.

The new moon comes every twenty-eight days. This meant that there were thirteen months in the Babylonian year. They always celebrated the spring season with a great feast.

The Babylonians were the first to use money made of gold and silver.

The Babylonians used weights and measures in doing business. Sometimes they counted by twelve. When we use the words "dozen" and "foot" we are using Babylonian measure. In this system they often counted things by sixty. When we say there are sixty seconds in a minute, and sixty minutes in an hour, we are still using the Babylonian system of counting.

Babylonian buildings. There was very little stone in the valley between the two rivers. So the buildings were made of clay. The Babylonians formed the clay into the shape of bricks. Then these were baked in the sun or over a fire. Many tall buildings were made by placing one story on top of another. But each new floor of the building would be smaller than the one beneath it. The floors were connected on the outside by a ramp or sloping pathway.

The Assyrians conquer Babylon. You know that the Babylonians lived in the southern part of the river valley. They were in constant danger of attack from the north as there were no mountains there to protect them.

The people who lived in the northern part of the valley were called Assyrians (as-si′-ree-ans). Their chief city was Nineve (nin′-eh-veh). They rode into the land of the Babylonians on horses and in chariots. They used iron weapons, fireballs, and battering rams. The foot soldiers of the Babylonians had no chance to conquer their powerful enemies. Thus Babylonia was captured by the Assyrians.

The Assyrians are conquered. Some time later another ancient people entered the valley between the two rivers. These people had moved up from their homes along the Persian Gulf. They were called Chaldeans (kal-dee′-ans). They defeated the Assyrians and destroyed Nineve, their capital city.

The Chaldeans rebuilt Babylonia, and for a while there was contentment in the valley. Because of the Chaldean victory, Babylonia is sometimes called the Chaldean Empire.

In the new empire there was a very famous king. His name was Nabuchodonosor (nab-you-koe-don′-owe-sor) who was a great soldier and builder.

The Hanging Gardens of Babylon

You will find stories about this king in your Bible History. He went to the country of the Hebrews and captured many of these people. He had them brought to Babylon where he treated them very cruelly. It was during his reign as king that Daniel, the prophet, was cast into the lions' den. Can you remember the rest of the story about Daniel?

One of the seven wonders of the ancient world was built by Nabuchodonosor. It is called the "Hanging Gardens of Babylon." He built these famous gardens for his queen who wanted to see flowers and trees around her home. The building itself was built just like Babylonian buildings.

The Chaldean Empire falls. Babylonia lost its power again after the death of Nabuchodonosor. Another country, Persia, overcame the entire valley between the Tigris and the Euphrates Rivers. By this victory, Persia became the owner of all the culture and civilization of the Chaldean Empire. Persia then learned how to use all the wonderful gifts that the Babylonians had discovered to make herself powerful.

5. Phoenician Carriers of Civilization

A nation by the sea. On the western shore of the Mediterranean Sea there is a small strip of land. It is surrounded by mountains and desert. It lies between Egypt and Babylonia. This land was called Phoenicia (fe-nish'-a) and the people were called Phoenicians (fe-nish'-ans).

Sea roads to Europe. The Phoenicians could not make a living by farming. Their land was too close to the sea and not suitable for this use. On the western side of this land lay the Lebanon Mountains. The wood from the cedar trees on these mountains was very fine. It made excellent ships. So the Phoenicians made many kinds of ships, some of which were moved by oars. Others were driven by the wind.

The Phoenicians spent much time fishing in order to secure food. They were the first known to use the North Star as a guide for sailing at night. Since they were good sailors, they had courage to sail far away from home. Soon they were visiting Egypt, Babylonia, Greece, Italy and Spain. In this way people in Europe learned better ways of living. Because the Phoenicians brought civilization back and forth from various countries, we call them the carriers of civilization.

Crafts of the Phoenicians. There were two good harbors in Phoenicia, in the cities of Tyre and Sidon. Tyre was famous for making purple dye. A shepherd discovered this dye as he was tending his sheep. One day the shepherd's dog was eating a shellfish. The shepherd was surprised to see a reddish-purple liquid coming from the dog's mouth. At first the shepherd thought it was blood. Then he saw that the liquid came from the shellfish.

Soon men found out that this liquid could be used to dye cloth. This dye became very valuable. It was so expensive that only kings could buy it. Perhaps this is why kings dressed in purple robes.

The city of Sidon was famous for making glass. Glass mirrors and glass beads were very precious. They were used instead of money in trading.

Ask your teacher to tell about the time time Our Lord mentioned the cities of Tyre and Sidon as He was talking to His disciples.

The Phoenicians as traders. The Phoenicians built colonies along the shore of the Mediterranean Sea. One very important Phoe-

Phoenician writing

nician colony was Carthage. It is on the northern shore of Africa.

The Phoenicians also built trading posts in different cities. At these trading posts they would trade their glass products and their rich purple cloth. They had other products of the East also for trade. The people of these cities would bring hides, grain, or metal for exchange.

The most valuable gift of the Phoenicians. The Phoenicians learned about Egyptian writing. Then they made up a set of letters, each of which represented a sound. This is called phonetic (foe-net'-ik) or sound writing. This set of letters is called an alphabet. It had twenty-two letters and was very much like our own alphabet. There were no vowels in the Phoenician alphabet. It was simpler than picture or wedge-shaped writing. It spread to other lands through the Phoenician traders.

Ancient carriers of civilization. We owe much to the Phoenicians because they were the carriers of civilization. Their most valuable gift to us is the alphabet.

Each man depends upon his neighbor in many ways. God uses some men to carry the gifts of one country to another so that all men can share them. In this way God used the Phoenicians. This was God's plan for them.

Civilization. In this Unit we are studying about the very earliest of people who lived on the earth. Some of them you have heard about before. Most of them you will learn about for the first time.

These early people did not live the same as we do today. Their homes, their meals, their clothing were very different. They had a much simpler way of living than we have today.

When we talk about a way of living we mean *civilization.* Ask your teacher to pronounce this word for you. Afterwards, you will learn to pronounce it yourself.

Many of these early peoples developed new ways of governing themselves. In doing this, they gave the world much useful knowledge.

Learning New Words

surgery	nomads	empire	irrigation	papyrus	hieroglyphics
Pharao	ancient	pyramids	characters	ancestor	prehistoric
obelisks	sphinx	weapons	chariot	wedge	cuneiform
astronomy		code	famine		

Time for Discussion

1. Ancient peoples gave us many useful things. Which people do you think did the most for us?
2. What gift do you think was the most helpful?
3. Why did the buildings of the Egyptians last longer than those of the Babylonians?
4. If you had a choice of living in ancient times, with what group of people would you have made your home?

A Little Quiz

Number your paper 1 to 10. After each number, write the letter that is before the correct answer below.

1. Confucius taught his people to
   a. believe in no religion but his
   b. take part in government
   c. lead good lives
   d. love and study science
2. The first alphabet was developed by
   a. Egyptians
   b. Chinese
   c. Chaldeans

37

d. Phoenicians
3. The Phoenicians were famous as
   a. farmers
   b. astronomers
   c. traders
   d. lovers of warfare
4. Pyramids were made by the
   a. Babylonians
   b. Phoenicians
   c. Chinese
   d. Egyptians
5. The "Hanging Gardens" are found in
   a. China
   b. Egypt
   c. Persia
   d. Babylonia
6. Gifts of the Chinese to the world are
   a. sailors and traders
   b. compass and gunpowder
   c. irrigation, paper
   d. laws and astronomy
7. Hammurabi was a ruler of
   a. Chaldeans
   b. Chinese

c. Babylonians
d. Persians
8. Nebuchodonosor is famous because he
   a. made a "Code of Laws"
   b. taught people to lead good lives
   c. captured the Hebrew people
   d. was just and kind to all
9. If your father made purple dye in ancient times, in what country would you be living?
   a. Egypt
   b. China
   c. Babylonia
   d. Phoenicia
10. Why is the Rosetta Stone valuable?
    a. it was of precious material
    b. it helped to make the Tigris River famous
    c. it showed the world how to read hieroglyphics
    d. it proved to the world that Phoenicians had an alphabet

Something to Do

Can you fill in this chart? Your teacher will work with the class, and tell you on what pages you may find the answers. Copy this chart on your own paper first.

Name of Country	Famous Person	Important Gifts to Civilization
1. China		
2. Egypt		
3. Babylonia		
4. Phoenicia		

CHAPTER III

GOD'S PROMISES KEPT ALIVE BY THE HEBREWS

A few reminders. Man was made to know, love, and serve God. That is why all men feel a need for adoring some kind of god. After the fall of Adam, people began to adore false gods. Some people made the sun one of their gods. Others thought that the seasons of the year or animals were gods. An Egyptian Pharao, Amenhotep IV, (a-men'-ho-tep) was the only ruler who tried to lead his people to the worship of only one god. But even he was not sure that he was right. To know the one true religion man needs special teaching from God. God took care of this need for His creatures. He appointed one race of people to teach and preserve what man needed to know about Him.

1. Teachers of the True Religion

The first of all peoples to worship the *one true God* was the Hebrew people. These were the people that God chose to teach and preserve the true religion. They also preserved the promise of a Redeemer which was made to our first parents.

The early Hebrews were a nation of shepherds. They were descendants of Sem, the second son of Noe. Although they suffered very much from their enemies they still taught men to lead good lives. They were driven from place to place over the earth. Still they kept on telling others that there is only one true God.

2. Abraham Father of the Chosen People

The call of Abraham. Abraham lived about two thousand years before the coming of Christ. When we first read about Abraham in the Bible he lived in the city of Ur near the Euphrates River. One day God called Abraham and told him to move his family to a place called Chanaan (kay'-nan). In obedience

Abraham meets King Melchisedech

to God's wishes, Abraham took his family and flocks to this land. Chanaan is the land we call the Holy Land. It is south of Phoenicia.

Abraham was a holy man. God decided that the Redeemer would come from his tribe. Abraham is called the Father of the chosen people, because the Hebrews were chosen to preserve the true religion and Abraham was their head.

Great Hebrew rulers. Abraham was the first of the three great rulers of the Hebrew people. Isaac, the son of Abraham, ruled after his father. He was succeeded by his son Jacob.

God changed Jacob's name to Israel. After that, the Hebrews became known as *Israelites*.

The Hebrews were a very large family. We call the founders and rulers of large families by a special name. We call them *patriarchs*. Abraham, Isaac, and Jacob were three great patriarchs.

The patriarchs taught the Israelites many things about the one true religion and the coming of the Redeemer. God gave the Israelites *prophets* also.

Some of these men foretold the coming of the Redeemer. Both the patriarchs and prophets worked to keep the Israelites faithful to God and prepared for the Redeemer.

3. Punishment of the Israelites

When Jacob was ruler of Israel, a great famine came upon the land. The people had no grain for food. There was plenty of grain for sale in Egypt. So the Israelites traveled to Egypt to buy some for themselves. While they were in Egypt, some of them became very friendly with the Egyptian people. They settled down in Egypt and became rich and happy in their new home.

God had promised the Israelites many favors if they remained faithful to Him. But some of them copied the bad example of their pagan neighbors. They adored false gods and worshipped idols just like the Egyptians. God had to send them a punishment to make them obey His laws. This is what happened.

Sufferings of the Hebrews in Egypt. A very cruel Pharao became ruler in Egypt. He forced the Israelites to work very hard. They had to carry heavy stones and supplies long distances to make roads and canals.

Sufferings often bring people closer to God. All these sufferings made the Israelites turn to God in humble prayer. God listened to their prayers. He sent them a great man to lead them out of the land of Egypt. **A very great leader.** The man God sent to the Israelites was Moses. He is one of the greatest men in history. Moses was the first one to write down the story of mankind. He wrote about the things that happened to man since the beginning of the world. Moses also wrote the history of his own people. God told him to write all these things, and he carried out God's orders.

You can read about these things in the Holy Bible.

The Bible, you know, is the best written record of early times. It is divided into many parts. Each part is called a "Book." The history that God told Moses to write is in the first five books of the Bible. The part of the Bible that contains the history of the Hebrew people is called the "Old Testament."

4. God Gives the Commandments through Moses

The journey to Sinai. God sent

Jacob's Ladder

Moses to tell the Israelites that their prayers were heard. God would free them from their sufferings. The Israelites believed Moses and offered thanks to God for restoring them once again to His favor.

God sent Moses to the Pharao. Moses told him to free the Israelites or God would punish the Egyptian people. The Pharao did not free the Israelites because he refused to believe the words of Moses. Then God sent ten plagues upon the Egyptians. After that, the Pharao changed his mind. He commanded the Israelites to leave at once, and they quickly left Egypt.

Moses and his brother Aaron led the Israelites through the desert. They had much trouble along the way. At last they pitched their tents at the foot of Mount Sinai. The first thing they did was to praise God. They thanked God for showing His love for them by giving them food and drink in the desert. He had also made them victorious over their enemies.

The storm on Mount Sinai. Long ago God had promised Abraham that He would teach the

Israelites His true laws. The time had now come for God to keep His promise. For three days the Israelites prepared themselves to receive God's instructions.

On the third day a great darkness came over the earth. There was thunder and lightning. This made the Israelites very much afraid. Moses was praying to God upon the mountain-top. The people could hear God speaking to Moses. They could hear God's voice speaking to them also and giving them the Ten Commandments. Moses came down from the mountain and told the people all that God had said. The people promised to obey all of God's commands as given to them.

The great gift of God to the world — His Laws. God called Moses to the top of Mount Sinai again. This time God gave him the Ten Commandments written on two tablets or pieces of stone. God did this to show that the Commandments must always be obeyed.

God gave other messages to Moses at this time. When you are older you will learn more about them. Among the things which God told Moses there was a special command. God com-

manded the Israelites to be a holy nation and to spread the knowledge of the promised Redeemer all over the earth. This knowledge was the greatest gift that any nation has given to the world.

Moses remained on the mountain for forty days. The Israelites thought Moses had forgotten them. They committed a terrible sin. They forced Aaron to make them a calf of gold. Then they adored and worshipped this golden calf as if it were like to God.

When Moses returned from the mountain he was angry. He was so angry with the people that he broke the stone tablets on which God had written the Commandments. He burned the golden calf. He punished those who led the people to adore this false god in place of the True God.

When the people saw this they began to do penance. Moses, too, asked God to pardon the sins of His people. God spoke to Moses. He told him to bring Him two new tablets. Upon them God wrote the Ten Commandments. He gave them to Moses again.

5. Israelites in the Promised Land

After the Israelites had been

Moses breaks the tablets of the law

at Mount Sinai for about a year, God told Moses to lead His people to the Promised Land. This journey took almost forty years. God had to punish the Israelites at times because they complained about the hardships they had to suffer on the way. The land God promised to Moses was the land we call the Holy Land.

As they came closer to the Promised Land, God called Moses to the top of Mount Nebo. He showed Moses the Promised Land from the top of this mountain. God foretold to Moses the time he was to die.

Now that time was near. Moses gave instructions to his people. He commanded them to be faithful to the worship of the one true God. He warned them about the terrible punishments if they disobeyed. But he promised them great blessings if they were faithful to God.

Kings for the Israelites. Israel was divided into twelve tribes. These twelve tribes became united under a king in a later period of Hebrew history. A man named Saul was the first king. The second king was David. He wrote beautiful songs, called *Psalms*, which are

The call of David

part of the Bible.

Solomon, the third king, built a great Temple in Jerusalem. The people of Phoenicia helped him to build it. Many of the precious objects in the Temple arrived in Israel on the fine ships of the Phoenicians.

A short time later the Kingdom of Israel was divided. Ten tribes broke away from the others and set up a kingdom of their own. They still kept the name *Kingdom of Israel*. The other two tribes settled in the south of Palestine. Their new kingdom was called the *King-dom of Juda*. The place where they lived was called Judea (joo-dee'-a). These people remained faithful to authority. It was from the Kingdom of Juda that Christ, the Redeemer, would come to the world years later.

At one time many of the people of Juda were taken to Babylon as slaves. They were later freed by the Persians. These people had conquered the Babylonians.

Faithfulness of the Jews. We owe much to the Jewish people. They kept alive in the world the promise of a Redeemer to come. They gave us the knowledge of the one true God. At times they fell away from God's Law. But through the prophets, they returned to the practice of the Commandments. From their lives we can learn that faithfulness and obedience to God is the pathway that leads to freedom and true happiness on earth.

New Words to Learn

plagues   patriarch   prophet   tablets   appoint   idol
hardships   psalms   famine   pagan   Israelites   Jewish

Some Work to Do

1. Write three sentences telling what the Hebrews gave to civilization.
2. Find in this chapter the paragraph that tells what the Phoenicians did for the Hebrews. Write on your paper the page on which you found it.
3. Ask your teacher to let you read in your geography or other books about people in other lands who still adore the sun or certain animals. What can we do to help them to know the true God?
4. In your own words make up a prayer. Ask God to send more missionaries to pagan lands. In the prayer thank God that you have been brought up as a Catholic.
5. When Moses came down from the mountain, he told the people to be faithful to God, and keep God's Commandments. Pretend you were one of the people in that group. Write down in your own words what Moses told the people.

Look It Up

Below there are five statements that are not complete. Copy them on your paper. These statements are taken exactly from the chapter. Find them and complete these statements by copying them from the textbook.

1. God changed Jacob's name to _____.
2. Moses was the first one to _____.
3. When Jacob was ruler of Israel, _____.
4. God commanded the Israelites to be a _____.
5. God had to punish the Israelites at times because _____.

46

Making Sure of Our Knowledge

1. Your teacher may help you to make a scrapbook showing the different things created by God during the six days.
2. Prepare a little play. You will pretend you are a Jewish boy or girl, or someone from one of the other countries studied in this Unit. Prepare one or two sentences to tell the class about your country when it is your turn to take part in the play.
3. Bring to class pictures of pyramids, the "Hanging Gardens," or an early kind of irrigation. Tell the class what these things mean to you.
4. Find on the map the following places: Egypt, Babylonia, Euphrates River, Nile River, Palestine, China, Phoenicia.
5. Hold a radio program. During the time of the performance, introduce Confucius to the class, if you are the announcer. At another time, introduce Hammurabi, Nabuchodonosor, Abraham, Noe, and Moses. Be sure that the pupils taking these parts tell the important things these people did so as to spread civilization.

Review of the Highlights of Unit One

1. All men are brothers in the same family, with Adam and Eve as their first parents.
2. Sin destroyed the plan that God had made for the world.
3. No race and no people can claim the goods of the earth for itself alone.
4. Jealousy and hate cause unhappiness in families and wars in the world.
5. Christ taught us to help our enemies as well as our friends.
6. Each man depends upon his neighbor in many ways.
7. God uses some people to carry the gifts of one country to another so that all men can share them.
8. The knowledge of the true God is the greatest gift that any nation has given to us.
9. Faithfulness and obedience to God is the pathway to freedom and true happiness.
10. Sufferings often bring people closer to God and make them ask for His help in their prayers.

Mastery Test for Unit One

I. Can you answer these questions? Number your paper 1 to 10, and write your answers after each of them.

1. Who were killed at the time of the great flood?
2. What river makes the soil of Egypt rich and fertile?

3. What is the name of Egyptian writing?
4. What race of people were forced to work hard for the Egyptians?
5. What helped men to read Egyptian writing after a long time?
6. Name the kind of paper made by the Egyptians.
7. Who led the Hebrews out of Egypt?
8. What early people were called carriers of civilization?
9. Who was the first king of Israel?
10. Which country gave us the alphabet closest to the one we use today in writing and speaking?

II. Matching Test. On a piece of paper copy the words in Column A. Write beside them the statement which makes them correct.

Column A	Column B
a. history	a kind of Babylonian writing
b. prehistoric times	kind done by the Egyptians
c. picture writing	story of what men have done in the past
d. famine	a shortage of food
e. cuneiform	when no records were kept in writing

III. Copy these sentences as far as the parenthesis. Then complete the sentence by taking from the parenthesis only the part which is correct.

1. The last kind of writing to be made by ancient peoples was (picture writing, sign writing, sound writing, cuneiform).
2. The rulers of Egypt were called (kings, monarchs, emperors, Pharaos).
3. Hammurabi is noted for (sculpture, building temples, collecting laws, fishing).
4. King Nabuchadonosor built the (Tower of Babel, pyramids, ark, Hanging Gardens).
5. The great Chinese teacher was (Hammurabi, Moses, Abraham, Confucius).
6. The people who had knowledge of the one true God was (Chinese, Hebrew, Egyptian, Phoenician).
7. The Hebrew king who built a temple at Jerusalem was (Saul, Solomon, Moses, David).
8. The man known as the "Father of the chosen people" is (Noe, Abraham, Moses, Jacob).
9. The kind of writing which was used by the Babylonians was (picture writing, sound writing, hieroglyphics, cuneiform).
10. The capital city of Assyria was (Babylon, Jerusalem, Ninive, Thebes).

IV. Completion Test. Choose the correct word to complete the following sentences.

purple dye alphabet weights and measures kings   sphinx
glass   crops   Tigris and Euphrates mummies   plagues
fire   traders   the Holy Land   life after death Chanaan

1. The most important thing the Phoenicians gave us is the _____.

2. The discovery that helped man to protect himself and improve his food was _____.

3. The Promised Land to which Moses led his people was _____.

4. After a while, the Hebrews began to be ruled by _____.

5. The land called the Holy Land today, in the time of Abraham was called _____.

6. One of the statues of stone built by the Egyptians is called _____.

7. Egyptians placed food in their tombs because they believed in _____.

8. Babylonians were the first to use _____.

9. The Phoenicians were great _____ with other countries.

10. The city of Tyre is noted for its _____.

11. To punish the Egyptians, God sent them _____.

12. Egyptians called the preserved bodies of their dead by the name _____.

13. The two rivers between which the Assyrians and Babylonians lived were _____.

14. Because of the Nile River overflowing its banks, Egyptians had rich _____.

15. The Phoenician city of Sidon is important because of its work in _____.

V. Number your paper 1 to 10. Answer Yes or No after each of the following questions.

1. Was the Garden of Paradise made for Adam and Eve?

2. Did early men use the English language?

3. Did God have a beginning?

4. Did Noe save many things in the ark?

5. Were Egyptian tombs called sphinxes?

6. Did the Chinese invent gunpowder?

7. Did the Babylonians divide the year into months, weeks, and days?

8. Did papyrus come from the Lebanon Mountains?

9. Were the Chinese inventors of cuneiform writing?

10. Did the Hebrews keep alive the promise of the Redeemer who was to come and save the world?

49

Hymns to Mary

HISTORY OF HYMNS. In teaching music, the notes are often called do, re, mi, fa, sol, la, and ti. These syllables are found in a Latin hymn to St. John the Baptist. This hymn was a petition to St. John to purify our lips so that we might sing the praises of God. What could be more appropriate when we practice singing? The first syllables of succeeding words in this hymn began with "do-re-mi-fa-sol, etc." Each of these syllables was on the next higher note of the scale. Guido d'Arezzo (980–1050), a famous choirmaster and monk, made known this helpful way of naming the notes of the scale and it is still in use.

ORIGIN AND MEANING. "*Ave Maria!* O Maiden and Mother," like some other hymns, was written by a Sister who preferred that her name be unknown. The only identification we have for the writer is the name, "Sister M." The hymn appeared first in "St. Patrick's Catholic Hymnal in 1862," in London. Like the writers of many of the medieval Latin hymns the only reward this author wanted was the praise given our Lord and His Mother.

Ave Maria! O Maiden, O Mother
Star of the Sea

Ave Maria! O Maiden, O Mother,
Fondly thy children are calling on thee,
Thine are the graces unclaimed by another,
Sinless and beautiful Star of the Sea!

Ave Maria! the night shades are falling,
Softly our voices arise unto thee,
Earth's lonely exiles for succor are calling,
Sinless and beautiful Star of the Sea!

Ave Maria! thy children are kneeling,
Words of endearment are murmured to thee;
Softly thy spirit upon us is stealing,
Sinless and beautiful Star of the Sea!

Ave Maria! thou portal of Heaven,
Harbor of refuge, to thee do we flee:
Lost in the darkness, by stormy winds driven,
Shine on our pathway, fair Star of the Sea!

APPLICATION. Mary is the Morning Star, heralding the dawn of each new day. We are all given daily an opportunity to turn to Mary. All of nature responds to the dawn of day. Is it not obvious that in prayer and devotion, we daily seek the help of Mary.

Courtesy of Rev. J. B. Carol, O. F. M.

UNIT TWO

CIVILIZATION DEVELOPS

UNIT TWO

CIVILIZATION DEVELOPS

IN UNIT ONE we learned that the Hebrews gave the world the greatest gift of all. This gift was the knowledge of the one true God and the hope of a Redeemer to come.

This Unit takes us farther west than the land of the Hebrews. It tells us the story of other peoples who passed on gifts of civilization. These peoples gave the world many valuable gifts in the period just before the birth of Christ our Redeemer.

One of these peoples was the Greeks. Their land borders on the Mediterranean Sea but it is broken up into many parts. Mountains and bodies of water form natural boundaries for this scattered country and help to protect it.

Above all other things, the Greeks loved liberty and freedom. They believed in freedom of speech and government by the people. The freedom we enjoy today had its beginnings in early times. The Greeks were one of those peoples who were FOUNDERS OF FREEDOM.

The Greeks lost their freedom because they quarreled among themselves. It is easy for a people to be conquered when there is no strong bond of union among them. But their gifts to the world were not lost. The nation that conquered them made good use of the gifts of the Greeks. That nation was Rome, a nation strong enough to establish peace.

At last peace reigned in the world. It was during this period of peace that Jesus Christ, the Prince of Peace, was born.

CHAPTER I

GREEK CHILDREN—SOLDIERS OR SCHOLARS

The two cities. The geography of Greece had a big part to play in making its history. In addition to the mainland, Greece is made up of many little islands. These islands are sometimes called the stepping stones from Asia to Europe. Many cities in Greece were separated from their neighbors by water or high mountains. Each city made its own laws and had its own way of living. This chapter tells about the kinds of training that children received in two of these important cities, Sparta and Athens.

1. Greek Beginnings

Early Greek families. Civilization was brought to Europe from Asia and Africa by the Greeks. In the beginning the Greeks were a very simple shepherd folk. They were not one race but a mixture of races from Asia and Africa. These people had moved from place to place looking for food for their flocks. Families of these shepherds traveled slowly in rough carts drawn by horses. They traveled southward on the west side of the Black Sea. Often many families joined together forming large groups called *tribes*.

On the Aegean Sea there is a peninsula which is cut up by mountains and bays. Many of these tribes settled there. Frequent wars broke out between them. Sometimes a conquered tribe was joined to a victorious tribe. Sometimes the defeated tribe joined another defeated tribe. At other times the defeated tribe would move away.

2. Formation of City-States

Independent city-states develop. The life of these people was not very happy. As wandering tribes they had no real government and no form of written laws. They had leaders who only settled their quarrels. These leaders became their heads in time of war.

But after hundreds of years the Greeks began to change their way of living. The tribes settled down and the land was divided among families. The men cared for the flocks. The women cultivated the fields. Little villages grew into cities which formed governments of their own. Soon these cities became powerful. They began to rule over the people who lived out in the country. Such cities were called *city-states*.

Life in the city-state. Each city-state had its own leader and made its own laws. It had its own army and honored its own pagan god. The Greeks taught their children to be loyal to their own city-state.

The Greeks thought far more of their own city-state than of the country of Greece. Each city-state was independent. We have forty-eight states in one big country. The Greeks had seventeen different states, but each of these was like a country in itself. Each city-state in Greece was jealous of other city-states.

The most important of these city-states were Sparta and Athens. They were great rivals.

Athens loved new and beautiful things. Sparta loved old and useful things.

3. Training of a Spartan Boy

Trained warriors. The people who lived in Sparta had come from the North some time before. They conquered the people who lived in Sparta and made them till the soil. They made slaves of still other peoples whom they captured in war. The Spartans feared that these slaves might some time rebel and turn on them. For this reason they trained their children to be good warriors and patriotic citizens.

The Spartan rulers taught that a Spartan boy did not belong to his parents but to the state. He could live with his parents only until he was seven years old. Then he went to live with other boys in a training camp.

Training was very severe. The Spartan boy had to learn to endure hardships. He slept without coverings on straw or on low bushes by the river bank. He was not allowed to wear shoes.

A Spartan boy was given very little food to eat. He was encouraged to steal food in order that he might learn to

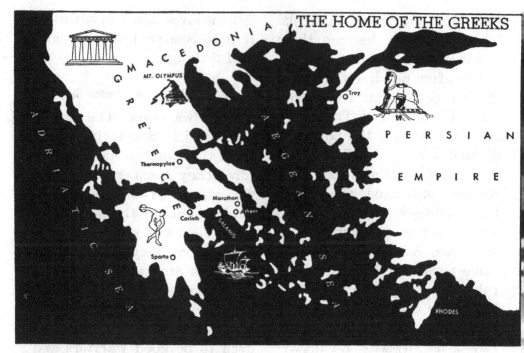

take care of himself in war. If he was caught stealing he was severely punished. The strange thing was that he would be punished for being caught, not for stealing.

Why was it wrong to punish a Spartan boy only because he was caught stealing? Why is stealing wrong, even if no one knows about it?

The Spartan boy was trained to jump and wrestle, to carry arms, and to use a shield and spear. He learned to read so that he could read the laws of the state. He did not learn to write. His whole education taught him to obey orders, endure pain, and win battles.

When a boy grew up he could not leave the army until he was thirty years old. Even then he could not be a merchant or a workman because he had to be always ready to defend his country.

Mother of a Spartan warrior. The Spartans thought that training the mind was almost unnecessary. The Spartan girl received about the same kind of training as the boy. The reason of this was that she was to become the mother of Spartan warriors.

The Spartans believed that everyone should have a strong body and be healthy and brave. The girl was taught to hate a

56

coward and admire a brave man. The fierce spirit of the women made the men do daring deeds for their country.

Sparta was a city of soldiers. The other tribes of Greeks respected the Spartans as soldiers. They took them as their leaders when they were in danger. The Spartan motto was "Come home from war *with* your shield or *on* it." That meant win or die.

One day a Spartan mother was told that her five sons had been killed in battle. She asked, "Did the Spartans win?" When told they had, she said, "That is what counts. Let us give thanks to the gods."

From this story we can see what was wrong in Spartan training. We know that man was created to do other things besides fight. Man has not only a body; he also has a soul. He is not just a citizen of the state. He must love and obey God, Who is above the state. If he does not, his life will not be full and happy. He will be only half a man.

The Spartans were the best soldiers and athletes of Greece. But these people did little to make the world happier or wiser. However, they gave us an example of great courage and patriotism.

Even in the world today, there are countries in Asia and Europe which are not much better than Sparta. Their rulers do not believe that *God is above the state*. They think that man is just a servant of the state. Can you find out the names of some of these countries? Can you name their leaders?

4. Training of an Athenian Boy

Athens — an ideal city-state. Athens was the most important city of Greece. It is near the center of Greece. It was built on a steep hill as a protection. The people of Athens were called Athenians (a-thee'-nee-ans). They were brave soldiers but they were interested in many other things besides the art of war.

Some of these people were farmers and shepherds. Others manufactured glass, pottery, leather, and metal goods. Those who lived in the city were mechanics and merchants. Those near the sea were fishermen or daring sailors. They sailed to lands as far west as Spain. By trading with people of other lands they grew rich and powerful.

The Athenians always loved freedom. Athens was the first

Athens today

great republic of the world. All her citizens could take part in making the laws. The Athenians had to serve the city in peace and in war.

The Athenians trained body and mind. The Athenian schools were ruled by the state, but parents had to pay to send their boys to school. The boy left home about daybreak. Each boy was given a slave who went with him to school. This slave was called a *pedagogue.* The slave carried his master's books. The books were really scrolls, and the slave carried them in a basket. The Greeks also wrote on wax tablets with a *stylus,* or pointed stick.

The boy was sent to two schools. In one he was trained to become a soldier. In this school he learned to handle a spear and a shield. He was taught also to wrestle and cast the javelin. Running, leaping, and ball-playing were part of the things he learned in this school. These things helped him to become a good soldier. They made his body strong and graceful.

The Athenians believed that the mind should be strengthened as well as the body. Their motto was "A sound mind in a sound body." How does this motto compare with the way the Spartans trained their children?

In the other school, the young boy was taught to sing and play musical instruments. The Athenians thought it was noble to love music. Art was part of his training as well. The Athenian boy also studied reading, writing, and arithmetic. These subjects he learned together with music in school.

The Athenians trained boys to be citizens. At fifteen years of age a boy went to a higher kind of school, called a *gymnasium*. There he learned to be an athlete. He took part in games with boys from other schools. He was taught above all things to behave and obey. Why was this a good thing in his training?

Much training was given in storytelling and public speaking. Athenians loved to talk and *debate* with one another and learn what was new. Many of the great poets and artists of Greece were Athenians, not Spartans.

Studying New Words

Athenian	warriors	patriotism	pedagogue	stylus
debate	citizen	gymnasium	javelin	peninsula
Spartan	wisdom	scholars		

What Is Your Score?

Number your paper 1 to 10. After each number write the letter before the correct answer.

1. The Greeks had which kind of government?
   a. an empire
   b. individual city-states
   c. tribal government
   d. a monarchy
2. The Spartan city was a city of
   a. merchants
   b. sailors
   c. soldiers
   d. scholars
3. Girls were trained in Sparta because
   a. people respected them

   b. they wanted training of mind
   c. Sparta wanted them to be trained as mothers of soldiers
   d. both mind and body of both boys and girls were trained in Sparta
4. In Athens, a boy's education was paid by
   a. the state
   b. school men
   c. parents
   d. the army

5. Spartans trained their citizens because they
   a. believed in training the mind
   b. wanted lawmakers for the city
   c. were afraid their slaves would rebel
   d. wanted them to take part in government
6. A peninsula is
   a. land surrounded by water
   b. land almost surrounded by water
   c. a small body of water
   d. water surrounded by land
7. The word "pedagogue" meant
   a. a school to train citizens
   b. an Athenian slave
   c. rule of the people
   d. Spartan kind of government

8. The Athenians believed that
   a. a few should rule
   b. all citizens should take part in government
   c. there should be no city-states
   d. boys should not be trained as citizens
9. Subjects studied in the Athenian school were
   a. reading, writing, geography
   b. history, spelling, reading
   c. reading, writing, arithmetic
   d. drawing, spelling, history
10. Which Greek city trained both mind and body?
   a. Sparta
   b. Tyre
   c. Athens
   d. Babylon

Mottoes of the Greeks

1. Explain the meaning of: "Come home from war with your shield or on it."
2. Tell whether your school is training you to have "a sound mind in a sound body," like the Athenians. Do you think the Athenians received a better kind of training than you received in a Catholic school?

Things to Talk About

1. What was wrong with Spartan training?
2. Should people live to serve the state, or should the state help the people?
3. Why is it wrong to break any Commandment, even if you are not seen by anyone doing the wrong thing?
4. Compare the way you live every day with the life of a Spartan boy or an Athenian boy.
5. Why was it more pleasant for a boy to live in Athens than in Sparta?

CHAPTER II

A glimpse of the chapter. In Unit One you learned that the Babylonians took the Hebrews away from their own country. They made them slaves in Babylon. These Hebrews had to stay in Babylon a long time. Finally, another country conquered the Babylonians and set free the Hebrews. That country was Persia.

Persia did not conquer Babylonia alone. Assyria, Phoenicia, and Egypt fell into her hands. That means that Persia owned all the land westward to the Mediterranean Sea. Can you find this on your map?

Still Persia was not satisfied. Persia had her eye on Greece. She prepared for a long time before finally setting out to war on that land.

This chapter tells the chief events of that war between Greece and Persia. It also explains about the great period of history which is known as the "Golden Age of Greece."

1. The Greeks at War

The Greeks were filled with fear. They learned that the Persian King and his army were coming to attack Greece. Already the Greeks who had been living on the coast of Asia Minor had been defeated by the Persians.

Fierce enemies. Greeks from Athens and Sparta united to fight the Persians. The enemy had a huge army and plenty of supplies. At first the Persians were victorious because they came from a powerful empire.

The Persians called their ruler the Great King. It was hard for a Great King to rule so many people. But the Great King built up a group of secret police that kept informing him about every important thing that went on in his empire.

Persia's Great King was named Darius (da-rye'-us). He

The Battle of Marathon

sent a very large army across the Aegean Sea to attack the Greeks. About twenty-six miles from Athens the two armies met. This was at a place called Marathon.

It was the Athenians who fought this battle. Sparta promised to help but did not send her soldiers. Spartans were superstitious people. They were afraid to set out before the full moon. The Athenians decided not to wait for them.

On the day of the battle the Athenians formed lines on the mountains around the plain of Marathon. They rushed down upon the Persians in a surprise attack, in spite of the terrible odds against them. Many of the Persians who were near the sea were drowned. Those who were not killed by the long Greek spears fled from the place of battle. The Greeks won. This was almost five hundred years before the birth of Christ.

One of the Greeks who fought in this all-day battle was sent to Athens to tell the good news. He ran all the way. As soon as he cried "Victory" he dropped dead. Have you ever heard a race called a marathon?

Persians return again. Ten years

later, the Persians tried again to conquer Greece. King Xerxes (zurk'-seez), son of Darius, de-decided to march overland to victory. He also sent ships to carry supplies. The ships would stay close to the shore as his army marched on land. He had to cross only one narrow strip of water, called the Hellespont. Xerxes built a bridge across this waterway.

The Persians had no trouble until they came to a narrow pass between the mountains and the sea. This place was called Thermopylae (ther-mah'-pi-lee).

There were only three hundred Spartans holding this narrow mountain pass. Their leader was Leonidas (lee-on'-i-das). Because they were so brave they were able to hold off the Persians until the Greek cities had time to prepare for battle. They stood their ground. However, there was a traitor among them. He showed the Persians a secret path which would take them behind the Greeks. There was no chance then for the brave Spartans. They fought until every man was killed.

A great victory. The Persians went on, quite certain of victory. They burned the beautiful city of Athens to the ground.

The city itself was deserted by the Greeks before the Persians arrived.

But the Athenians were not conquered. They had a good navy and a very fine leader. This leader was Themistocles (the-mis'-toe-kleez).

You will remember that the Persian ships carried all the food and supplies, while the army marched on land. West of Athens and a little to the south there is a body of water. It is called the Bay of Salamis (sal'-a-miss). All the huge Persian ships sailed into this narrow bay and were trapped there by the Greeks.

The Persian army was left without food and supplies. They could not fight in such a small place with their big ships. The Greeks won a great victory at this time. It was in the year 480 B.C. Do you know what "B. C." means?

The Battle of Salamis was one of the most important battles of the world. To the Greeks it meant that Persia was defeated. To the world it meant that all the Greek ideas of freedom and democracy would not be lost. They would be passed on through the years to come. Where did our country get its first ideas of ruling itself?

Brown Brothers

The Battle of Salamis

2. A City Rebuilt

All the Greeks rejoiced in the defeat of the Persians. At once, they began the great work of rebuilding the city of Athens. They planned to make it more beautiful than ever.

The Acropolis. In the center of Athens there is a steep and rocky hill. The name of this famous hill is Acropolis (a-krop'-owe-lis). To the Athenians it was the most wonderful spot in the world. Beautiful marble steps led up to the top of this mountain.

On this hill the Greeks erected temples, statues, and altars. It was really a sacred place to them. You know, of course, that the Greeks believed in many gods. They did not believe in the one true God as the Hebrews did. They thought their gods lived on a mountain called Mt. Olympus.

One of the Greek gods was named Athena (a-thee'-na), the goddess of wisdom. It was in honor of this goddess that the Acropolis was decorated. At the entrance to the Acropolis was an especially beautiful statue of Athena. It was the work of the greatest of Greek sculptors, Phidias (fid'i-as).

The Parthenon. Phidias and his pupils built a temple on the mountain in honor of Athena. This small but very beautiful building was called the Parthenon (par'-the-non). The columns were very graceful and the carvings so beautifully made that they seemed alive. Many of the Greek ideas and forms can be found in some of our modern buildings.

The columns of Greek buildings were perfect in form but not large. The simplest column was called the Doric. Although it was plain, it was beautiful. A taller column but lighter and more slender, was called the Ionic. This one had curved lines at the top of the column. Have you ever seen buildings with Doric or Ionic columns?

The Greek theater. On one side of the hill of Acropolis there was built a large theater. It was an outdoor theater where plays were given in the daytime. It had been built in the form of a semicircle. Rows of seats were on the hillside.

The Greeks loved poetry and used to learn it by heart. They read over and over the poems of Homer, a blind Greek poet of long ago. Homer's chief poems are the *Iliad* and *Odyssey*. They tell stories of early

Philip Gendreau, N. Y.
On the Acropolis

wars between Greeks on the peninsula and Greeks in Asia Minor, at Troy. The *Odyssey* tells of the travels of a Greek hero after the war was over.

The Greeks liked to watch plays acted on the stage. They were the first to do this. We received this idea from them. These plays told stories about their gods or great heroes. That is why they made a theater on the sacred hill of the Acropolis.

The Greeks wanted all their citizens to learn the great lessons taught by their plays. So if anyone was too poor to afford the small price for attending, the state paid his way.

Another idea we received

Brown Brothers

A Greek theatre. Would this remind you of a modern stadium?

from the Greek plays is that of having a chorus on stage. The Greek chorus was large and they sang or recited together. They would explain parts of the play when no scene was taking place. At other times they were really part of the play itself.

3. Great Leaders of Greece

Pericles. Very shortly after the defeat of Persia, Athens chose for its leader a wise man named Pericles (per'-i-klees). Under his rule Athens became a very famous and important place. At this time there began a period of history known as the Golden Age of Greece. It is called the Golden Age because it was a time of great peace and happiness for the Greek people. It lasted from 479 to 431 B. C.

During part of this time Athens was guided by Pericles. Some people call this time the "Age of Pericles."

Greece gave many gifts to civilization during this time. Some of these gifts are beautiful architecture, good government and love of wisdom.

Pericles was a truly great man. He wanted Athens to be the leading city in every way. He often asked the people what they thought about certain things he was going to do for the city. The people kept him as their leader for thirty years.

Freedom in Athens. Freedom, you know, is one the great gifts of God to man. But God gave freedom to every man who is born into this world. Everyone, then, has the right to enjoy the blessings of freedom.

The people in Athens showed their love for freedom by the way they governed themselves. All citizens were free to take part in the government. There is a special name for this kind of government. Two Greek words, when combined as one word in our language, mean "rule of the people." This English word is *democracy*. You have often heard this word used by others and you will understand it better when you are older.

Athens was the world's first city to be ruled as a democracy. This was the greatest contribution of the Athenians to the world — democratic government. We who live in this great land of freedom must remember what we owe to the Greeks. The Greek ideas of freedom have been handed down to us. We can truly say that these people were one of the FOUNDERS OF FREEDOM.

How democracy worked in Athens. The group of people which actually governed Athens was an Assembly and a Council. Members of the Assembly were elected by the people. Leaders were chosen by means of voting in a public place.

The Council consisted of fifty men from each of the tribes of Greece. It was so arranged that each tribe would rule for seven weeks.

The officials, or elected officers, would call a meeting in a public place to propose or suggest a new law to the people. The people were paid for attending these meetings and fined if they were absent.

Any citizen who wished to speak in public for or against a law could do so. Those who could speak well were called *orators*. The best speaker had the most power. Pericles became a powerful leader because he could think clearly and speak well.

Weaknesses of Greek democracy. The democracy of Athens was limited. Everyone in Athens could not vote. There were many slaves in Athens who had no rights. They had to work like animals. Often they were not treated as human beings or persons. These slaves were not allowed to vote on anything.

There were people in Athens who came from other countries. These also could not vote or take part in the government of Athens in any way, as they were not citizens.

In Greece one could not become a citizen unless his parents were citizens. In our country even people from other lands who come here to live may become citizens if they follow certain rules laid down for them. Slavery ended in our country a long time ago. Democracy in America is more truly a "rule of the people" than was the democracy of Athens.

We know that democracy is not simply a kind of government. It is also a way of thinking and living. It must be built on respect for other men because they are our brothers. We are all children of God. The people of Athens did not have this true idea of democracy.

Colonies of Greece. The Greeks showed their love of liberty in another way. They gave great freedom to their colonies. As soon as a colony was formed it governed itself. It was never again subject to the city-state. To the Greek, his own city-state was his fatherland. He would gladly die for it, if necessary.

Greece had some trouble in keeping her liberty, just as some countries in the world today. Sometimes a rich and powerful man would seize the government. He would then force other citizens to obey him. Such a man is called a *tyrant*.

Some tyrants were good and ruled well after they had gained power. The Greeks, however, did not like any ruler who was not elected by all the citizens.

Draco. Draco, one of the rulers, was asked to do something of great importance. The citizens asked him to put the code of laws in writing. They knew the people would like this for they would feel protected. This was the first time that Greece had any written laws.

After this time, a ruler could no longer change a law to please himself. The laws were so severe that they were said to be "written in blood." People were put to death for small offenses.

Solon. In 595 B.C. Solon (so'-lon), another lawmaker, wrote a new set of laws. Solon's laws gave everyone, rich and poor, equal rights in justice. Murder was punished by death, but small offenses were no longer punished by death. Solon said that happiness did not come from riches but rather from a good conscience and right conduct.

Solon was good to the poor. He cancelled the debts of all the Athenians. He forbade anyone to sell another person into slavery. What do you think about this law and why do you agree with Solon's idea?

Even the poorest class was given a share in the government during the time of Solon. Because of his just laws Solon was called the great lawmaker of the Greeks.

4. Wise Men of Athens

Athens was the home of great thinkers and wise men.

Solon

Socrates

They were constantly looking for knowledge in order to be wise. We call such men by the name philosophers (fil-ah'-so-fers). This word comes from the Greek language and means lovers of wisdom, a most suitable name for these men.

These philosophers taught other men by talking to them in the market place, in a shop, or even while walking along the street. They taught people not to tell lies about their neighbor. They also taught them to suffer harm rather than be dishonest, and to seek peace in all things. The Greek philosophers also taught people to honor old age, obey all laws, and to be willing

Plato

Brown Brothers

is famous for his way of asking questions.

Some people did not like Socrates because he showed them that they had made mistakes. They accused him of not paying proper respect to the gods of the city. For this reason they said he must die. His friends tried to save him, but he refused to let them do so.

Plato. Some philosophers taught in beautiful parks and gardens. One of these was Plato. He called his garden the *Academy*. Plato was first a pupil of Socrates. Plato taught about government and rules of conduct. Plato believed in life after death and worked out a plan for an ideal government.

to face punishment if they broke the law.

The most famous Greek philosophers were Socrates (sok′-ra-tees), Plato, (play′-toe), and Aristotle (ar′-is-totl).

Philosophers of Athens. Socrates was one of the greatest of these philosophers. He taught that it is true wisdom to do what is right. Although he was a very ugly-looking man, many people loved him and wanted to imitate him.

One of Socrates' teachings was: "Know thyself." He had his own way of teaching people how to think correctly. He did it by the kind of questions he would ask the people. Socrates

Aristotle

Brown Brothers

Aristotle. The greatest of all these wise men was Aristotle. He went on voyages so that he could add to his knowledge. He laid down rules of good government. Aristotle wrote about science, poetry, conduct, and grammar. His writings have been studied by pupils and teachers all through the years up to now. Aristotle's school was called the *Lyceum* (lye-see'-um).

These philosophers were called wise men. Yet even the mind of a wise man is not as great as the mind of God. Unless God teaches man, man makes mistakes.

Aristotle became the guide of many later philosophers. Some of these were Christian thinkers, such as St. Thomas Aquinas, who lived many, many years later.

Aristotle's ideas. Today our ideas about many things are like the ideas Aristotle had. But we know more about some things than Aristotle did. Aristotle's ideas about God were not as complete as ours are today. This is because Aristotle did not know about Christ.

As you know, Jesus Christ is true God and true Man. When He came on earth, He taught many things about His Heavenly Father. He told us about the Holy Trinity. This means that there are three Divine Persons in God. Aristotle never knew this. He knew that God exists, but he did not know that there are three Persons in God. That is one reason why we say that Aristotle's ideas about God were not as complete as ours.

Later on, we shall see how Christ's coming changed the whole world.

Words for Mastery

philosopher	tyrant	colonies	statesmen
traitor	officials	orators	

Points for Discussion

1. Why was Pericles a great leader?
2. In what way do we enjoy more freedom than the Greeks?
3. Prove this statement: "Happiness does not come from riches but from a good conscience and right conduct."

Can You Study by Yourself?

Find the answers to these questions in your text. Write each answer in complete sentences.

71

1. Why is a very long race called a marathon?
2. Why did the Greeks regard attendance at plays as part of their religion?
3. How did the Persians find out another way to get into Greece besides Thermopylae?
4. What is the difference between the Doric and Ionic columns?
5. Why was the Golden Age of Greece important?

Testing for Knowledge

Try to get a perfect score of 15 on this short test. On a sheet of paper write the items in Column A. Next to each, copy the letter in Column B which best matches it.

Column A	*Column B*
1. Pericles	a. first Greek philosopher
2. Socrates	b. wrote first laws of Greece
3. Aristotle	c. greatest of Greek philosophers
4. Draco	d. the lawmaker of Greece
5. Solon	e. Athenian statesman and leader

Do the same with these items.

6. Marathon	f. where Pericles ruled
7. Thermopylae	g. one of greatest battles of the world
8. Salamis	h. a narrow pass where Spartans fought
9. Athens	i. Athenian victory by surprise attack
10. Acropolis	j. mountain sacred to the Greeks

Do the same with these items.

11. tyrant	k. betrays his country
12. orator	l. one who seizes the government
13. philosopher	m. enjoys rights and duties as a result of living in a state
14. citizen	n. searches for knowledge to be wise
15. traitor	o. one who speaks well and with power

CHAPTER III

ALEXANDER SPREADS GREEK CULTURE

A truth to be lived. All men have certain God-given rights, one of which is the right to liberty. We have seen that the Greeks had a great love for liberty. However, they sometimes forgot that real liberty means the freedom to do what is right. Sometimes they failed to allow this liberty to others.

In this chapter we shall learn how Greece fell into the hands of another nation. Fortunately for the world, the new ruler of Greece loved Greek learning and customs. This chapter tells how this ruler spread Greek knowledge and mingled the customs of other lands with it.

1. How the Greeks Failed

Greece is weakened. The Greeks were not united. Each city-state was jealous of the others. When one city-state was attacked others would join together to drive away the enemy. But when the war was over they would break apart again. Because of this, the Greeks did not become a strong nation.

When Athens became rich and powerful, Sparta made war upon her and defeated her. Sparta then became the leading city-state.

Yet Sparta's power did not last long. She was conquered by Thebes, another Greek city-state. All the Greek city-states fought so many wars that they became very weak. This made it very easy for a foreign enemy to attack Greece.

Rise of King Philip. North of Greece there lay a small country called Macedonia (ma-se-doe'-nee-a). People of this country spoke the same language as the Greeks and worshipped the same gods. Yet these people were a separate nation.

This country had a very famous king, Philip II. He had great hope of one day conquering other lands and making his own land very famous. The first thing he did was to train his soldiers for warfare. He built up the largest army in the world at that time.

Demosthenes. There was one great orator in Greece who was watching closely all King Philip's preparations for war. This great orator was Demosthenes (de-mos'-theh-nees). He knew that Greece would be the first country Philip would attack. Therefore, Demosthenes gave many fine speeches. He warned his people that they would soon be at war with the Macedonians. Because these speeches were written against Philip, they are called "Philippics" (fi-lip'-iks).

Demosthenes was not always a good orator. In the beginning he could not even speak distinctly. But he made up his mind to overcome this fault. He placed some pebbles in his mouth, and practiced speaking in this way. Thus he learned to speak and pronounce every word distinctly. After some time, he became the best orator in Greece.

Greece is defeated. The Greeks, however, continued to fight among themselves. They did not pay much attention to the warning of Demosthenes. Fi-

Brown Brothers
Demosthenes

nally, the Macedonians marched against the Greeks. Then the Greeks remembered what Demosthenes had said. It was too late now. Soon all Greece came under the complete control of Philip.

Greece under King Philip. This new ruler of Greece was a wise man. He did not destroy the fine buildings and works of art which he found in Greece. He did for the Greeks what they did not do themselves. He united the Greeks and asked them to help him conquer the Persians. This they agreed to do because the Greeks and Persians, you know, were enemies.

Before Philip completed his

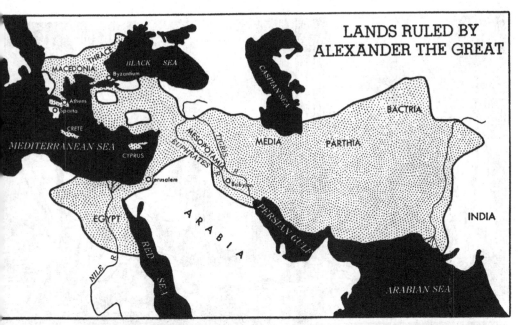

LANDS RULED BY
ALEXANDER THE GREAT

plan, he died. His son, Alexander, became king. He was then twenty years old.

2. Alexander—Master of the Known World

Alexander the Great. Alexander had received an excellent education. Aristotle, the great teacher, had given him the best instruction possible. Aristotle gave his young pupil a great love for Greek art and literature.

Even as a boy Alexander could do things other boys were unable to do. He could tame very swift and wild horses. In fact, he did not fear to do anything.

Alexander loved to study about ancient heroes. He loved especially the heroes that Homer wrote about in his poems about wars. He could recite these long poems by heart.

Defeat of the Persians. Alexander was determined to carry out his father's plan. He gathered a small army of brave and well-trained soldiers, and set out for Persia. The Persian people had no real love for their country because they had no share in ruling it. Alexander led his army across rivers and mountains. He stopped at nothing until he conquered every Persian city.

Ruler of the world. Alexander did not stop at Persia. He marched on to distant India. Every country which had been ruled by Persia was conquered

Aristotle teaching Alexander

by him. Before he was thirty years old, Alexander became the ruler of the civilized world.

3. Greeks As Teachers of Other Nations

Greek ideas are spread. Wherever Alexander went he built new cities. In every city which he conquered, Alexander left companies of Greek soldiers. In this way people of other lands learned Greek ways of living and culture.

Thirty thousand Persian soldiers were given a Greek soldier's training. Alexander then admitted them to his army.

A new Greece. The people who received this Greek culture and learning were the Persians, Babylonians, Phoenicians, and Egyptians. All these people, except the Egyptians, lived in lands called the *Orient,* or East.

The Greek soldiers, in turn, learned how the people in the East lived. These soldiers brought back to Greece the customs of the Orient.

The rule of Alexander brought changes in Greek civilization. Now Greece had the culture of the East mingled with her own ways of living. Before Alexander, Greek culture was called *Hellenistic* (hel-len-is'-tik). These big words you will understand better when you study ancient history in high school.

Death of Alexander. The ruler of the civilized world was a very vain man. He wanted himself to be worshipped as a god. Whenever other people did not agree with his ideas, he became very angry.

He died suddenly at the age of thirty-two. History calls him Alexander the Great.

4. Spread of Greek Language and Culture

Center of Greek learning. The most famous city built by Alexander was that of Alexandria in Egypt. This city had a good harbor. The ships of many nations came there to trade. At this city the traders learned about Greek art and learning. Students from other lands came to study from the Greek teachers at Alexandria. Much of our knowledge of science and mathematics comes to us from them.

Words for Study

science   Orient   foreign   literature   instruction   control

For Discussion

1. Why was it easy to conquer the Greek nation?
2. How was Greek culture spread to other lands?
3. How did Greece develop a new culture after Alexander's rule?

Checking Up on Your Study

Fill the blanks with the correct answer. Write your answers on another paper.

1. A great Athenian orator who warned the Greeks against Philip was _____.
2. Liberty is a gift given to ____ at birth.
3. The Greek city-states were not united because _____.
4. King Philip conquered _____.
5. Persia was conquered by ____.
6. Aristotle's famous pupil was _____.
7. The center of Greek learning was the city of _____ in Egypt.
8. For a while, _____ became the leading city-state.
9. "Philippics" was the name given to speeches made by _____.
10. North of Greece was the country of _____.

CHAPTER IV

THE FOUNDING OF ROME

A city on seven hills. Few countries of the world are more beautiful than Italy. It is a peninsula extending into the Mediterranean Sea. It is farther west than the land of the Greeks. The Apennine Mountains are like the backbone of Italy. They run almost north and south through the land. On either side of them lie beautiful plains and valleys. These are made fertile by the waters of the Tiber and Arno Rivers. Find Italy on your map. It is easy to recognize because it is shaped like a boot.

The Tiber River is on the western side of the Apennine Mountains. Not far from the sea stand seven hills on the Tiber River. It was at these seven hills that the great city of Rome grew up.

Rome today is a place dear to the hearts of all Catholics. The Pope, the Vicar of Christ on earth, is the Bishop of Rome.

But Rome was not always a home of Christians. It is a very old city. In ancient times it was the home of pagan people. These people adored false gods as the Greeks did.

In this chapter you will learn about the beginning of the great city called Rome.

1. Roman Beginnings

You have read above that Rome was founded on seven hills. This happened about a thousand years before the birth of Christ. A group of people came from the north and settled on the plain near the seven hills. The region itself was called Latium (lay'-shi-um), so the people called themselves Latins. After these Latin tribes made Rome their city, they were called *Romans*.

How Rome got its name. It is interesting to know how Rome received this name. According to an old story there was a king who had twins named Romulus and Remus. They had a wicked uncle who wanted to become the king. He put the babies in a little cradle and stole them from their father's palace. He let the cradle float down the Tiber River, hoping that the twins would be drowned.

The cradle with the twins was washed ashore. A wolf took care of them until a shepherd found them. They grew up to be strong men. With help from other men they built a city on the Tiber River.

When it came time to name the city the twins quarreled. Each wanted to name it after himself. In the quarrel Romulus killed Remus. He then became the first king of Rome. This story is called a legend. A legend is a story that is partly true, but partly made up.

Rome had six kings after Romulus. The last was called Tarquin (tar'-kwin) the Proud. He was so cruel that the Romans drove him away. Then Rome refused to have any more kings as rulers. This happened about the year 500 B.C.

The heroes of Rome. The Romans had many other legends about their heroes. We know, however, that many of the early Romans were brave and patriotic. They had many war-like neighbors. Soon the Romans conquered their enemies, and Rome became the strongest city in Italy.

The legend of Horatius. One of the Roman heroes, called Horatius (ho-ray'-shi-us), is supposed to have lived about the time of the cruel King Tarquin. When Tarquin was driven away from Rome, he asked some people to the north of Rome to help him fight to get his kingdom back. He set out with an army to recapture Rome.

Outside the city of Rome there was a narrow wooden bridge. The Romans decided to cut down this bridge to keep

Horatius at the bridge

Culver Service

Brown Brothers

The Roman Senate

After Rome had driven out King Tarquin, it started another kind of government. It was called a "republic." This word comes from Latin and means "public business." Our country is a republic but it is much different from the first republic of Rome.

The Romans now began to choose their own rulers. They gave the duties of their kings to two men. These men they called consuls. A consul was elected to serve for one year. A group of noblemen, called the Senate, helped the consuls to rule Rome.

In order to be elected consul, one had to be a wealthy person. Rich people had special privileges. They claimed they were the only ones who should have power. They said their fathers founded Rome. For this reason they were called *patricians* (pa-trish'-ans). This word comes from the Latin for "father." All members of the Senate were patricians.

There was another class of people in Rome at this time. They were the common people, or the poorer class. This class was known as the plebeians (ple-bee'-ans), because the

Tarquin out. There was not much time to do it. In the meantime, a brave man named Horatius, and two other soldiers, were fighting back the enemy on one side of the bridge.

Just as the bridge was ready to fall, the two soldiers ran back to the Roman side of the bridge and were saved. Horatius was left behind on the other side. Quickly he jumped into the Tiber River and swam safely to shore. Tarquin and his army were forced to turn back. Rome was saved by the bravery of Horatius and his helpers at the bridge who are admired even today for their bravery.

Latin word for common people is "plebs." They were Roman citizens as well as the patricians. But no plebeian was allowed to vote or take part in the government. No plebeian could ever be allowed to marry a patrician. This shows that the patricians thought themselves much higher than the plebeians. Do you think God wants people to have ideas such as this?

The soldier hero. In time of war the Romans appointed one man to rule the city. They called this man a dictator. No dictator could rule for more than six months.

During one war a man named Cincinnatus (sin-sin-ay'-tus) was named dictator. A long time before, he had been a consul and a senator. At this time he was living on his farm in the country. Cincinnatus was plowing his field when a messenger came to tell him about his appointment. He dropped his plow, and hurried to Rome immediately. At once he ordered all men who could carry a

The Romans ask Cincinnatus to command the army

weapon to follow him. In the dark of night he marched upon the enemy. It took Cincinnatus only sixteen days to defeat the enemy.

The Romans wanted Cincinnatus to continue as their leader. But he felt he was no longer needed. He left Rome, and went back to his work on the farm, without looking for praise or reward.

The plebeians struggle for their rights. The market place and trading center of Rome was called the Forum. The people often gathered there to talk over public affairs. The plebeians often met in the Forum to demand their rights. They said they would build a city of their own if they were not treated fairly. They very often disturbed the peace by their complaints.

Because the plebeians threatened to set up their own city, the patricians gave in to them, little by little. The struggle between the two classes lasted about a hundred years.

Finally the patricians al-

The Roman Forum. The Twelve Tables of the Law were set up here

lowed the common people to choose men to represent them. These men were called tribunes (trib'-yoons). They were allowed to stand outside the Senate to hear what was going on. The tribunes had the right to shout "Veto" when the Senate attempted to pass an unjust law. This word means "I forbid." After this call, such a law could not be passed.

Written laws. It was good for the people to have tribunes. Yet even this did not give full protection to the people. There were no written laws. Since the patricians could explain the unwritten laws any way they pleased, there was not always the same justice for everyone. So the plebeians demanded that laws be put into writing.

The laws were then written on twelve bronze tablets called the "Twelve Tables of the Law." They were set up in the Forum for everyone to read. Every schoolboy had to memorize these laws. Thus, the people came to know the laws. They learned what their rights were and what they could demand in justice.

3. Roman Rule Extends to all Italy

The Gauls take Rome. The story of Rome at this time is a story of many wars among the people themselves. Such wars are called civil wars. The Romans became so weak from these wars that they almost lost their freedom.

The Gauls, a greedy tribe from the north, attacked Rome and burned the city. They forced the Romans to pay a large amount of gold to get back their ruined city. The Romans never forgot this defeat.

Rome gains more land. The Romans learned a good lesson from the war with the Gauls. It was a lesson that the Greeks failed to learn. The Romans knew now that a nation must be united in order to grow strong. They stopped quarreling. At once they worked together and started to rebuild their city, making it greater than it had been.

The Romans had as neighbors towards the north a group of people called Etruscans (e-trus'-kans). These people taught the Romans many things. They taught them how to use the arch in building. The Etruscans were good people in carrying on business, too.

However, the Romans feared these people. They had a powerful army to defend themselves. The Romans waited until the

A main road in Roman times

Etruscan army was fighting other enemies. Then the Romans began slowly moving into the Etruscan towns and cities.

Roman power grows. Rome now began to grow to the east, north, and south. Greek cities south of Rome saw this city getting powerful. But they were not strong enough to fight Rome. They had no choice but to fall under Roman rule. Soon Rome had defeated the Gauls, Etruscans, and all other tribes of Italy. This was about 275 B.C.

Rome rules Italy. The Romans became rulers of all Italy. They wanted to rule wisely and well. They decided that they would make some of the conquered peoples citizens of Rome. This plan worked well. So they gave more and more of their new subjects the privilege of becoming Roman citizens. Did the Greeks and Romans have the same idea of citizenship? How did the two ideas differ?

Rome built many good roads at this time. These led to the cities and colonies that had been captured. In this way the Romans could reach their new lands more easily. The roads also helped trade to develop between Rome and her colonies. **Rome and her colonies.** When the Romans conquered a new land they ruled it according to Roman law. They allowed the people many freedoms. Sooner or later the people began to adopt Roman ways of life. They even began to use Latin instead of their own languages.

This is one reason why Latin became widely used in the world.

In the next chapter we shall see how the Romans came to rule the whole world.

For Discussion

1. How did the plebeians force the patricians to give them their rights?
2. If you had lived in Rome in the days of the Republic, what privileges would you have had? Which would have been denied to you?

Word Study

colonies	patrician	veto	dictator	Forum
tribunes	plebeian	consul	republic	

Test

Copy the statements below on a piece of paper. Write "True" or "False" after each statement.

1. Rome is said to have received its name from Romulus.
2. Early Rome was governed by kings.
3. The Roman people sent away Tarquin the Proud.
4. The plebeians could be elected consuls.
5. The tribunes protected the rights of the common people.
6. Veto means "I forbid."
7. The patricians were the poor people.
8. Horatius was an enemy of the Romans.
9. The written laws of Rome were called the "Twelve Tables."
10. The Romans had to buy back their city from the Gauls.
11. The Forum was a place where patricians demanded their rights.
12. The Etruscans taught the Romans how to use the arch in building.

CHAPTER V

ROME BECOMES MISTRESS OF THE WORLD

More victories for Rome. Rome had become ruler of all Italy. She was growing more powerful all the time. But Rome still had a great enemy outside Italy. That enemy was a rich and powerful city in Africa, called Carthage (kar'-thij). Neither city wanted the other to be more powerful.

Rome fought three great wars with Carthage. That city had been founded long ago by the Phoenicians. These wars are called Punic wars, because "Punic" comes from the Latin word for Phoenician.

These wars lasted one hundred and twenty years. After these wars Rome was the victor.

Rome did not stop conquering lands. Every land the Romans knew about became a part of Rome, or a Roman Province. Everywhere Romans went, they spread all the culture they learned from the Greeks. They built great roads that led from Rome and reached to all their provinces. Have you ever heard anyone say, "All roads lead to Rome?"

Rome became rich from the wars of many years. This was not good for the Roman people. Dishonest men made Rome a very unhappy city.

This chapter tells the story of the Punic Wars. It tells of the troubles that came to Rome as a result of her great victories. It shows how the republic of Rome failed to govern the world. It proves that riches, power, and wealth are not the things that can make people happy. You know the right answer. Happiness is found in keeping God's laws and always doing His holy will.

1. Rome and Carthage at War

In Unit One you learned that the Phoenicians built up much trade with other lands and started colonies in other lands. One of Phoenicia's most important colonies was Carthage, on the northern coast of Africa.

Carthage was even more important than Alexandria. It had a very powerful navy. Later it broke away from Phoenicia and became a city governed entirely by itself. Carthage owned two islands, named Corsica and Sardinia. These islands are very close to Italy. Can you find them on your map?

Near the toe of the boot of Italy there lies a larger island, called Sicily. This, too, belonged partly to Carthage. Rome did not like to have any land owned by Carthage so close to its land. Carthage was a powerful city and Rome was afraid Carthage might some day take some more land for itself.

Carthage did just what the Romans did not like. Not only a part of Sicily, but now the entire island was taken by Carthage. The Romans prepared for war immediately. The First Punic War was about to begin.

The fight for Sicily. Carthage had a very fine navy, but not a good army. The people of Carthage had a strange idea about soldiers. The Carthaginians themselves did not want to fight on the battlefield. They hired soldiers to do the fighting for them. Meanwhile, the Carthaginians went about their own affairs in the usual way. You know what a difference this made in battle. These hired soldiers had no love for Carthage. They were not fighting for love of country, so they did not fight very well.

The Romans, on the other hand, had a very fine army. Their soldiers were well-trained. Besides, they had a great love for Rome. This love for their country helped make them better soldiers.

EARLY ITALY

The Roman Army prepares for battle

Rome built a great fleet of warships so as to attack the ships of Carthage on the Mediterranean Sea. The sailors fought as bravely on the decks of their ships as the soldiers fought on land.

The war lasted for twenty years. Finally, Rome won. Sicily now belonged to Rome. This was the first land outside Italy which Rome gained for itself.

Elephants on the Alps. Peace lasted for only twenty-three years. Then a great general named Hannibal (han'-i-bal) arose in Carthage. Hannibal's father taught him to hate the Romans. He took an oath that he would never be friendly to them. Was it right for him to do a thing like this?

Hannibal had one great ambition. He wanted to capture Rome. He would overcome all hardships in order to do this.

Hannibal set out from Spain, where Carthage had a colony. He had with him many horses and elephants. These animals would march right in through the enemy lines in time of battle. What do countries use today in place of elephants?

Brown Brothers

Hannibal leads his army across the Alps

Hannibal brought his army overland from Spain to Italy. Most of the time he remained close to the coast. However, along the way he had to climb the high mountains called the Alps. It was a very dangerous journey. Would you like to climb the Alps on the back of a huge elephant?

Hannibal's failure. For fifteen years Hannibal traveled up and down Italy capturing lands here and there. Yet he never captured Rome. The Romans hoped he might become discouraged. But Hannibal was determined to succeed.

Then the Romans did something to stop Hannibal. They sent an army to fight Carthage. Hannibal left Italy quickly. He hastened to save his beloved city. But finally Rome defeated Carthage.

A brave leader of the Romans at this time was named Scipio (sip′-i-owe). It was he who drove Hannibal's army out of Spain. However, he was not so great a leader as Hannibal, his enemy.

These ruins are part of a theatre of old Carthage

At the end of this Second Punic War, Carthage lost her possessions in Spain.

The burning of Carthage. The Romans did not help the Carthaginians after the war was over. Instead, they were looking for an excuse for another war. They said, therefore, that the people of Carthage were making weapons for war. This was the cause of the Third Punic War.

This time the Romans really destroyed Carthage. The city was burned to the ground. Then the Romans sowed salt in the ground so that not even grass would ever grow there again.

All the lands owned by Rome in the West were formed into a province. It was called the Roman Province of the West. It continued to grow larger.

2. A Freedom Lost in Rome

Before the Romans had become such great conquerors, they led a simple, happy life. No one was too rich or too poor in Rome. Many Romans owned their own small farms. Everyone was able to make a living for himself. This is only right.

It is part of the freedom God gave to us.

Soon some of the Roman leaders became greedy for more land. These people took over the small farms that belonged to Roman citizens who were away at war. In this way one rich man could make one large farm out of several small ones. He could produce a great deal of grain because he had many slaves working for him.

The small farmers who still kept their farms found out they could no longer make them pay. The big, wealthy farmers were doing all the business. The people could not get jobs on the large farms because so many slaves had already been hired to do the work.

This was a sad condition. The city of Rome had become rich and prosperous. But many of her people had become very poor. The people of Rome had lost the freedom to earn a living. There were a few greedy men in Rome who kept all the wealth of Rome to themselves. This condition exists in many parts of the world today.

Evil practices in Rome. These poor men and their families gathered in the city of Rome. Here the government gave them some food to keep them alive.

This was not a good thing. The government became more important than the people.

By degrees the people began to have little love or loyalty for their city. The citizens lost respect for themselves and the government as well. Dishonest men tried to get high positions in Rome. They found it easy to obtain votes. Poor people received money from these men if they promised to vote for them. Was this a good plan? Would you take money from another on this condition?

Some Romans tried to help. Some wise Romans saw how bad these conditions really were. Two such men were brothers who belonged to the Gracchus family. The older brother was named Tiberius Gracchus (tie-bee'-ree-us grak'-us). He had been elected tribune. From this fact you know to which class of Romans he belonged.

Tiberius tried hard to get back farming lands for the poor people. To do this he made a law, which was passed by the Roman Senate. This law said that no man could own more than three hundred acres of public land. It also said that the state should rent the remaining land to the poor for a small rent. Rich men were not allowed to buy this land.

This law was not pleasing to the wealthy men. Before Tiberius could carry out his plan, he was killed by one of his enemies.

Gaius Gracchus. Later, his brother, Gaius (gay′-us) Gracchus, tried to carry out the plan. Further, he wanted to send some of the poor people out of Italy to settle new lands. He thought also that all the people of Italy should be made Roman citizens.

Many of the rich did not like the ideas of Gaius Gracchus either. A war broke out because

Cornelia and her sons

Brown Brothers

of this plan of Gaius, in which Gaius lost his life.

These two brothers, called sometimes the Gracchi (gra′-kee), did not succeed in helping the poor. We can still admire their bravery and courage in standing up for what is right and trying to help the poor people. Some day you too may be in a position like this. You will be even braver than they were if you ask Almighty God to help you.

A little story. When the Gracchi brothers were very young, a lady came to visit Cornelia, their mother. In those days Roman ladies were very fond of showing off their fine jewelry. "Cornelia," said the visitor, "please, may I see your jewels?" Cornelia called her two boys to her, and said, "These are my jewels." Can you tell why Cornelia was right?

3. Roman Culture

Rome was not satisfied until all the lands which Alexander had conquered had become Roman provinces. Greece, Babylonia, Persia, were no longer independent. Now no army was so strong as the Roman army. People in the conquered nations now became part of the great Roman army.

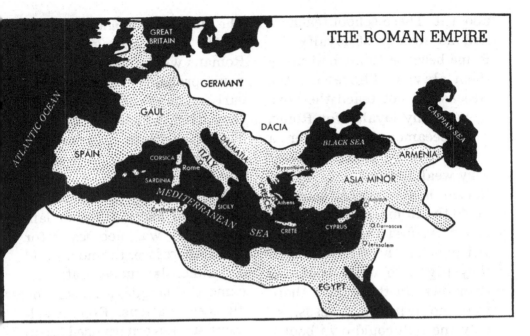

THE ROMAN EMPIRE

There was one land conquered by Rome which had better ways of living than Rome. In other words, it was a more civilized nation. That land was Greece, about which we have already studied.

When the Romans conquered Greece, they gained more than the land itself and its people. They discovered those wonderful gifts of civilization that the Greeks had. Not only that, but they brought them to Rome, and made them part of their own way of living.

Early Roman education. In early times in Rome, the boys were taught all they needed to know by their fathers. The girls received their training from their mothers. They did not have to attend school as you do.

A great change took place after the Greeks had been conquered. The Romans saw that these Greeks were cultured and intelligent. They brought Greek teachers to Rome so that the boys of Rome could receive a better education from them. But the Romans made slaves of these Greek teachers.

Now Roman boys were taught grammar, reading, public speaking, the Greek language and ways of thinking. Older boys were often sent to Athens to finish their studies.

It was good for the Roman boys to have such fine teachers. Only one thing was wrong about it. These school teachers had no feeling of loyalty for Rome because Rome had made them slaves. Therefore the Greeks did not teach the boys to have any loyalty for Rome. This became serious after a while. It made Rome finally a very weak nation.

Roman books. Greek learning made the Romans interested in books. At first they copied the writings of the Greeks. Then they began to write books of their own. In those days there were no printing presses, so only the rich could own books.

The author of a book would give his writing to a bookseller. This man hired clerks to copy it by hand.

A book in those days was not like any of your books. The paper of the book was either papyrus or parchment. Parchment is made from the skins of animals.

This paper was formed into a long sheet and rolled around two sticks, one at each end. When you have finished reading a page of your book, you simply turn the page. But if you were a Roman boy, you would unroll some of the paper from one stick and roll back some of the paper on the other stick at the same time.

The common language of the world. The language of the Romans was called Latin. This name probably came from the early name of the region where they lived, which was Latium. The Greek slaves gave the boys lessons in Latin as well as Greek.

The nations conquered by Rome had many different languages. It was necessary for them, therefore, to understand a common language. Latin became the language spoken by all these nations. Roman soldiers and governors used Latin in dealing with other people.

People do not use Latin today as their ordinary language. But in most parts of the world the Catholic Church uses Latin during her ceremonies. The priests in most parishes celebrate Mass in Latin. Boys who want to become priests must study Latin. The Church also uses other languages besides Latin in her services. Ask your teacher to tell you something about these other ways of saying Mass and praying.

Many of the words in our English language are really Latin words, or parts of Latin words. French, Spanish, and Italian are some languages that came from Latin.

Some Roman roads are still in use

Greek gifts become Roman culture. Greek treasures of art were brought to Rome. After a while, Roman theaters were built, similar to the Greek theaters. Greek athletes came to take part in many games in Rome. The people began to amuse themselves with Greek plays. Even the *Iliad* of Homer was translated into Latin and acted out upon the stage.

The Romans had their own gods which they worshipped. But even the Greek gods came to be looked upon as Roman gods. The beautiful homes of the Romans were decorated with Greek statues. Roman public buildings looked like Greek temples. The Romans used bronze coins for money. They exchanged these for the silver ones of the Greeks.

In commerce the Romans used weights and measures of the East, which the Greeks taught them. The Romans invented a system of Roman numerals. This system was easier to use than the Greek system. Your teacher will show you how to read Roman numerals, if you do not yet know them.

4. The End of the Roman Republic

The Roman republic had existed for over five hundred years before the birth of Christ. It was successful when Rome was a small city-state. But when Roman soldiers came back from war, they found that Rome was no longer a good place for plebeians to live. The rich people were ruling Rome. Poor people did not get a square deal. You have read how hard the Gracchi brothers tried to help the plebeians and how they failed.

The Romans no longer made sacrifices for Rome. They had little patriotism. Many of them lived in a dishonest and selfish manner. Much of the wealth of Rome was wasted in idle, useless amusements.

People could see that a change was needed. That change was a new kind of government. The republic was now very weak in Rome. The rest of this chapter tells you about the change that took place in Rome.

A leader appears. A man named Julius Caesar (see'-zer) became consul of Rome. After his term of office was finished, he asked to be made governor of Gaul. At that time the Romans had possession of only a small part of this country. The people of Gaul had once burned the city of Rome. Gaul was the land we now call France.

Caesar was a very ambitious man. He longed to win the entire country of Gaul for Rome. He collected a large army and finally defeated the Gauls after twenty years of fighting. In high school, some boys and girls read the story of the Gallic Wars in Latin. Does your big brother or sister study "Caesar"?

Caesar did not stop at Gaul. He conquered other people who lived on the other side of the Rhine River. We call that land Germany today. Caesar's army crossed over to Britain. Britain

Julius Caesar

Culver Service

Caesar's army fought very hard

is the older name for England. A famous saying of Caesar was: "I came; I saw; I conquered."

These great victories made Caesar very popular. News of his leadership spread to Rome and to all the provinces. But this fame was too much for some other men in Rome. They were jealous of Caesar, and disliked him very much. These people were determined not to let Caesar become powerful in Rome.

The Die Is Cast. Caesar was now ready to return to Rome. He heard that he had many enemies there. He had to decide on whether he would make war on his enemies in Rome or not. If he led his army across the Rubicon River which separated his province from others, then he would face his enemies. Caesar crossed the Rubicon, and then said: "The die is cast." Do you know what Caesar meant by this?

Caesar had two famous enemies in Rome, named Crassus and Pompey. He fought for five years before he finally overcame them. Now Caesar alone ruled Rome and its provinces. He was powerful because he had a great army behind him. The people wanted to make him king, but Caesar refused. They made him dictator for ten years. He is called "the greatest of the Romans." He was master of the whole Roman world.

What Caesar did. Caesar insisted that all men in office be just and honest. He tried to make some good laws. He granted citizenship to some of the conquered people. This meant they could have their law cases tried by Roman judges according to Roman law. In this way men could know that their rights would be protected in any part of the Roman Empire.

Caesar helped trade and agriculture too. He used the taxes or tribute money to build beautiful temples and public buildings. He arranged the calendar by assigning 30 days to some months, 31 days to others, and 28 to February, except in leap year. Can you guess which month is named after Julius Caesar? Many of the months are named after pagan gods of the Romans.

Death of Julius Caesar. Caesar made many changes in Roman life. Many people disliked him for the good he did. They thought he might be dictator for life, or would make himself king.

Even his closest friends went back on him. One day they plotted against Caesar. They thought they would be the next rulers if they got rid of him. Caesar was cruelly stabbed to death in the Senate. But his murderers did not get the power they wanted. The people turned against them and drove them from Rome.

A new government. After Caesar's death, there was more war to see who would become ruler. Finally, Caesar's nephew, called Octavian (ok-tav'-i-an), rose to supreme power. He then changed his name to Augustus. Before this, no one used this name except in speaking of the gods. He was called "Imperator" which means emperor. The land he ruled was called an empire. This was the beginning of a new government for Rome.

Emperors as gods. We see that Octavian called himself Augustus. He meant that he was to be treated as a god.

For many years after this, pagan Roman emperors were treated like gods. The people offered incense to them. They gave them other honors.

We shall see that the early Christians refused to treat the emperor as a god. They were willing to obey him as an emperor, but not as a god. For this reason many Christians were martyred.

Discussing What We Have Read

1. Why were not the laws of the Gracchi brothers put into force?
2. How did Caesar succeed in gaining control of Rome?
3. Why does the Catholic Church use Latin in her church services?

Word Study

prosperous   loyalty   parchment   empire   province   Imperator
agriculture

Map Study

Turn to the maps, pages 56 and 87. Find the following places on those maps. Write one sentence about each of them. Your teacher may give you the first column for today, and the second column tomorrow.

Mediterranean Sea	Carthage
Athens	Rome
Sparta	Sicily
Thermopylae	Tiber River
Macedonia	Apennine Mountains

A Game to Play

Copy the following names on your paper. Pretend that you are a radio or television announcer. Tell in four sentences the important things you know about the first person, etc. If you do this well, your teacher may select you to carry out this program as announcer for a parents' meeting.

Hannibal	Julius Caesar
Scipio	Augustus
Tiberius Gracchus	Gaius Gracchus
Pompey	

Reviewing the Entire Unit

1. The Greeks were one of the early peoples to have a high type of civilization.
2. There were two very important city-states in Greece, Athens and Sparta. Each one was a little state governing itself.
3. Spartan boys were trained to be good soldiers and warriors.
4. Athens had a democratic form of government. However, it was a limited democracy.
5. Athens had some men who were deep thinkers. We call them philosophers. Aristotle was the greatest of these men.
6. Athens loved beautiful things, and made beautiful buildings.
7. While Pericles was leader, the Golden Age of Greece began.
8. Greek learning was spread by colonists and traders to other countries on the Mediterranean Sea.
9. The Greeks defeated the Persians who attempted to conquer them.
10. King Philip of Macedon conquered Greece.
11. Alexander the Great conquered all lands on the western side of the Mediterranean Sea.
12. Knowledge of Greek culture spread to other lands during the time of Alexander the Great.
13. The Romans had seven kings before they formed a republic.
14. The Romans brought Greek civilization to Rome, developed it, and preserved it for the world.
15. Dishonesty and other evils were growing in Rome. No one could stop these things because the people in power were rich and wanted all the money for themselves.
16. Julius Caesar conquered Gaul and then fought his enemies in Rome. He became dictator of Rome, and tried to help the people.
17. After Caesar's death, quarreling followed. Finally, Caesar's nephew became ruler. He was called Augustus and was the first Emperor.
18. The Roman Republic fell. Rome became an Empire in 31 B.C.

To Help Your Learning

1. Write a paragraph in your notebook on the life of an Athenian boy; also paragraphs on a Spartan boy and on a Roman boy.

2. Plan a little play. Select one of the following topics for your subject. Your teacher will help you to find the part of this Unit that tells the

story, if you have not yet learned to use the index.

The Story of Roman Books
What the Gracchi Brothers Did
How Rome was Founded
The Greatest of the Romans—Caesar
Why We Call a Race a Marathon
What a Roman Boy Learned in School
The Great City of Carthage
Alexander's Empire

3. The class may prepare a frieze on various parts of Greek and Roman culture, such as Doric and Ionic columns, a Greek theater, Roman numerals, calendar of Julius Caesar, etc.

Mastery Test for Unit Two

I. Rewrite the following statements filling the blank with the correct answer selected from the list of words.

Julius Caesar	Alexander	Pericles	Augustus
Philip	Romulus and Remus	Tiberius Gracchus	Socrates
Homer	Horatius	Cincinnatus	Aristotle

1. Rome is said to have been founded by ——————— and ———————.
2. —— ——————— conquered Gaul.
3. The King of Macedonia, who conquered Greece, was ———————.
4. A great statesman and leader of Athens was ———————.
5. After Greece was conquered, the next ruler of Macedonia and the world was ———————.
6. ——————— was one of the most famous of the great Greek thinkers.
7. A Roman who saved his city by keeping back the enemy at the bridge was ———————.
8. ——————— was working on his farm when called to be dictator of Rome.
9. The first emperor of Rome was ———————.
10. ——————— was a blind poet of early Greece.
11. A tribune who tried to help the poor people of Rome was ——————— ———————.
12. The Greek thinker who was the greatest philosopher was ———————.

II. Number your paper 1 to 10. After each write the letter preceding the correct answer in the following exercise.

1. The surface of Greece is
   a. flat
   b. mountainous
   c. desert
   d. sandy

2. At Marathon the Greeks defeated the
   a. Egyptians   c. Babylonians
   b. Hebrews   d. Persians
3. The most beautiful building in the world is said to be the
   a. Greek home   c. Hanging Gardens
   b. Parthenon   d. Colosseum
4. "Veto" means
   a. the die is cast   c. sound mind in a sound body
   b. I forbid   d. rule by the people
5. What city was destroyed in the Punic Wars?
   a. Rome   c. Carthage
   b. Athens   d. Gaul
6. Besides the patricians, the other group of Romans was the
   a. soldiers   c. plebeians
   b. Spartans   d. statesmen
7. Julius Caesar became
   a. tribune   c. king
   b. dictator   d. plebeian
8. The general of Carthage who invaded Rome was
   a. Caesar   c. Hannibal
   b. Pericles   d. Leonidas
9. The Twelve Tables of the Law applied to
   a. Christians only   c. plebeians and patricians
   b. plebeians only   d. Christians and plebeians
10. Those who were the most civilized passed on their civilization to
   a. Greeks   c. Phoenicians
   b. Persians   d. Romans

III. After each number on your paper write "Yes" if answer is true, and "No" if false.

1. Greeks had good ideas about democracy.

2. Horatius' army crossed the Alps.
3. Roman boys were taught by Greek teachers.
4. Greek ideas never spread to other lands.
5. The Golden Age of Pericles was a time of great glory for Greece.
6. Government by the people is called a democracy.
7. The tribune represented the common people at the door of the Senate.
8. Rome is a city of Greece.
9. The Parthenon was built to honor Caesar.
10. Alexandria, Egypt was famous for Greek learning and culture.

IV. Match Column A with Column B. Place the correct letter after each number on another piece of paper.

Column A	*Column B*
1. Solon	a. a Roman dictator
2. Socrates	b. teacher of Alexander the Great
3. Phidias	c. lawgiver of Athens
4. Scipio	d. Roman general in Second Punic War
5. Plato	
6. Julius Caesar	e. a Greek philosopher who wrote on knowledge and truth
7. Leonidas	f. a Greek philosopher who was put to death
8. Aristotle	
9. Demosthenes	g. a great Greek orator
10. Themistocles	h. general in battle of Marathon
	i. general in battle at Salamis
	j. Greek sculptor

Do the same with these.

1. pedagogue	a. government by the people
2. parchment	b. government in Rome after Tarquin
3. tribune	
4. republic	c. Latin
5. common language of world	d. one who spoke for the common people
6. culture	
7. democracy	e. kind of civilization
8. city-state	f. made from skin of animals
	g. slave of an Athenian boy
	h. state which rules itself

Hymns to Mary

HISTORY OF HYMNS. The year 374 A.D. was a time of much trouble in Milan, Italy. The Arian heresy was causing this trouble. St. Ambrose, who became Bishop of Milan, was looked upon by the people as the leader who could restore order. The people became afraid that the heretics might harm their Bishop, and so they gathered about him in the church to protect him. While the people were there, St. Ambrose wrote hymns for them to sing. St. Ambrose not only wrote hymns, he encouraged others to write hymns too.

ORIGIN AND MEANING. "I'll Sing A Hymn to Mary" is one of the most popular English hymns to the Blessed Virgin. It was written by Father John Wyse, an Irish priest who was born in Dublin in 1825. The hymn became popular after it was included in a hymnal in 1862. In composing this hymn to Mary, Father Wyse has selected some of Mary's most famous titles, and he has used them in the first three stanzas. Singing this hymn is much like reciting the Litany of the Blessed Virgin.

I'll Sing A Hymn to Mary

I

I'll sing a hymn to Mary,
The Mother of My God,
The Virgin of all virgins,
Of David's royal blood.
O teach me holy Mary,
A loving song to frame;
When wicked men blaspheme thee,
To love and bless thy name.

II

O Lily of the Valley,
O Mystic Rose, what tree
Or flower, e'en the fairest,
Is half so fair as thee?
Oh, let me, though so lowly,
Recite my Mother's fame
When wicked men blaspheme thee,
To love and bless thy name.

III

O noble Tower of David,
Of gold and ivory
The Ark of God's own promise,
The Gate of Heaven to me,
To live, and not to love thee
Would fill my soul with shame;
When wicked men blaspheme thee,
I'll love and bless thy name.

IV

When troubles dark afflict me,
In sorrow and in care,
Thy light doth ever guide me,
O beauteous Morning Star!
So I'll be ever ready
Thy goodly help to claim;
When wicked men blaspheme thee,
I'll love and bless thy name.

APPLICATION. Mary was selected by God to be the Mother of Jesus, and we recognize her holy name.
All persons have a name dedicating them to a saint in heaven. A thought in your prayers will honor him, and get his help and intercession through Mary.

Courtesy of Rev. J. B. Carol, O. F. M.

UNIT THREE

CIVILIZATION IS CHRISTIANIZED

CHAPTER I—CHRIST, THE CENTER OF CIVILIZATION

The Golden Age of Rome
Christ, the Redeemer of the World
Christ, the Teacher of the New Law of Love
Christ, the Giver of Supreme Gifts
Christ, the King

CHAPTER II—ROME, THE CENTER OF CHRISTIANITY

Fearful Men Become Fearless
The Early Christian Church
Saint Paul, Hater and Lover of Christ
The Holy Spirit Guides the Church

UNIT THREE

CIVILIZATION IS CHRISTIANIZED

Christ, the Ruler of All Men. In your study of the Old World so far, you read about emperors, dictators, kings, and other men who ruled countries. All these leaders became famous for a time. Then their kingdoms passed away.

Do you know what these kingdoms are called? They are really *earthly* kingdoms. Everything we now see and enjoy will some day pass away, just as earthly kingdoms do.

The time had now come for the greatest event in history. All other events in history point to this. While Caesar Augustus ruled the world, Jesus Christ, our Divine Saviour, was born.

This new-born King was above all the rulers of the world. Although they did not know it, He was their Master and King. It was He who gave them authority to rule, and not they themselves.

Christ said He came to establish a Kingdom also. Christ did not mean that people would pay taxes to Him or go to war with other countries for Him. His kingdom is the kingdom of our souls. Our souls, you know, will never die, because they are spiritual. The spiritual Kingdom of God is one that will last forever.

You have seen that some of the ancient peoples had some idea of what freedom means. But God's becoming man gave the world greater freedom than anyone had ever before imagined.

Christ taught us what we must do to be free and happy.

CHAPTER I

CHRIST—THE CENTER OF CIVILIZATION

Christ—the Center of Time. Do you know why Christmas is such a wonderful time of the year for all Catholics? You know that it is the birthday of Our Lord and Savior, Jesus Christ. We celebrate Christmas because we have so much love and loyalty in our hearts for the Lord of heaven and earth.

The birth of Christ on earth was the greatest event in all history. In God's plan, Our Lord is the center of all things. He is the center of everything that has happened to the world. Christ should be the very heart and soul of our lives, too. Do you really love Him above all things?

You have studied in this history book many things that happened long ago. Every one of these things happened before Christ was born. These events were really preparing the world for this great day when the Redeemer of the world would be born. Whenever you read "B.C." after a date in your text, it means the period *before Christ* was born.

You are living "in the year of Our Lord" nineteen hundred —————. It is written "19—, A.D." The letters "A.D." mean "the year of Our Lord." These letters stand for the Latin words "Anno Domini."

In this chapter you will read about the greatest event in history. You will read how God fulfilled His promise to our first parents. God not only kept His promise of a Redeemer but gave the world greater gifts than anyone has ever dreamed or imagined. If the world will follow Christ, our Leader, people will have peace on earth and eternal happiness in heaven.

1. The Golden Age of Rome

In the second Unit, you learned about the little village on the Tiber River that became the city of Rome. In only seven hundred years it became strong enough to conquer all other nations of the civilized world. After the fall of the Republic, Caesar Augustus became the first Emperor. Augustus was a very clever ruler. He allowed the Romans to elect officials, but he kept all the power to himself.

Deeds of Augustus. Under this Emperor's reign, great things were done in Rome. Augustus encouraged education. He built many new buildings in Rome. These were much larger than the Greek buildings, although they copied the Greek styles of building. The dome was used, as well as the vaulted roof in buildings.

The Romans used to celebrate a great victory by building a great archway in Rome in honor of the victorious general. When such a general would return to Rome, he and his army would parade under this arch, which was named after him.

The Romans knew how to supply their cities with fresh water. The water usually came from far up in the hills. It was made to flow across valleys and streams on large structures called aqueducts (ak'-wi-ducts). These aqueducts were like high bridges. It took fourteen of these aqueducts alone to bring the city of Rome the water it needed.

The Romans also built some very large theaters. The stadium, called the Coliseum (kol-i-see'-um), seated 80,000 people. In the arena of this building trained men would fight with swords. These men were called *gladiators* (glad'-ee-ay-tors).

This was great amusement for the Romans. However, it was a very pagan way of entertainment. Often the people would tell the winner to kill his partner.

The goverment of the Empire. Augustus ruled all of Europe south of the Rhine and Danube Rivers, and the countries at the eastern end of the Mediterranean Sea. Egypt and the entire northern coast of Africa was also part of the Roman Empire.

Augustus ruled the Empire well. Each conquered country was made a Roman province. A governor ruled each province. The governor had men who told him what was happening in the various districts or provinces.

The Romans made wise laws.

An old Roman aqueduct. It is still in use

One famous one stated that a man is innocent until he is proven guilty. Judges, lawmakers, and lawyers put these laws in order so that all men could know them easily. This is what the great Roman thinkers did. Many nations have copied Roman ideas of law and government because these were so well drawn up. Roman ideas of law and government were the greatest contributions of Rome to civilization.

Peace in the Empire. Augustus disliked war. His reign was one of peace and order. It was the happiest and greatest age Rome ever had. Because of this, it has been called the "Golden Age of Rome."

The Empire of Augustus was not a perfect empire, however. The Roman governors were often unkind to their subjects. The people had to pay heavy taxes to Rome. Slaves were numerous in Rome and they were cruelly treated. Not all the people of Rome were wealthy. Some belonged to the working class, and others were very poor. In fact, the poor outnumbered the rich.

MOSES ON MT. SINAI

Through the ages, God's interest has been in the salvation of mankind and the betterment of man's lot. During the time of Moses, God desired to impart to him rules of life for the welfare of everyone. These rules are known as:

THE TEN COMMANDMENTS

1. I am the Lord thy God; thou shalt not have strange gods before Me.
2. Thou shalt not take the name of the Lord thy God in vain.
3. Remember thou keep holy the Lord's day.
4. Honor thy father and mother.
5. Thou shalt not kill.
6. Thou shalt not commit adultery.
7. Thou shalt not steal.
8. Thou shalt not bear false witness against thy neighbor.
9. Thou shalt not covet thy neighbor's wife.
10. Thou shalt not covet thy neighbor's goods.

The Emperor takes the census. Caesar Augustus was anxious to know just how many people were in his great Empire. So he sent out a command to the entire land. Everyone was told to report his name, age, occupation, and other information. We call this listing of people "taking the census." In our country, the census is taken every ten years.

In Palestine, this census was taken as the Emperor commanded. Everyone had to go to the city where his people had always lived. There he was enrolled with the rest of his family and relatives.

At this time, Mary was living at Nazareth in Galilee. She belonged to the royal family of David. The city of David was Bethlehem, about three days' journey from Nazareth. St. Joseph belonged to the tribe of David also. Mary and Joseph went to Bethlehem and obeyed the law of Caesar Augustus.

2. Christ, the Redeemer of the World

You recall that the Jews were God's chosen people. All through the years they kept alive the worship of the one true God. They waited and hoped for the coming of the Messias. They were sure that Christ the Redeemer would come when the world was at peace. One of the prophets had foretold this. Other prophets had predicted that Christ would be born in Bethlehem, laid in a manger, and wrapped in swaddling clothes.

While Mary was at Nazareth, the angel Gabriel appeared to her. He told Mary that she was to be the Mother of God. Mary was greatly frightened at this because she did not expect to be the Mother of God. The

THE LAND WHERE
CHRIST LIVED

angel told her not to be afraid. The Holy Spirit would perform this great work in her. Then Mary gave a truly great answer to the Angel. She said she was ready to do whatever God wanted her to do, because she was His servant. That is what Mary meant when she said, "Behold the handmaid of the Lord; be it done unto me according to thy word."

The birth of Christ. When Mary and Joseph went to Bethlehem some time later, the greatest event in the world took place. Jesus was born. God had planned to be born in Bethle-hem. Caesar Augustus did not know that he was carrying out God's plan. Because of the census, Mary and Joseph went to Bethlehem.

The name "Jesus" was given to the new-born Son of God. This lovely name means Savior. The word "Christ" means anointed, or selected for some special work.

The special work of Jesus was to save the world. Only God could do that. Man had offended God by sin. The gates of heaven were then closed. God came down to redeem us and open again the gates of

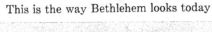
This is the way Bethlehem looks today

The birth of Our Lord

heaven. Because of this special work, we call Christ our Redeemer.

Throughout the years many holy men and women had prayed for the coming of the Redeemer. The story of ancient peoples is the story of man reaching out to find God. Since man could not come to God by himself, God came to man.

3. Christ, the Teacher of the New Law of Love

God had many lessons to teach us when He became man. Besides His Mother Mary and Saint Joseph, the first to see Him and learn His lessons were the shepherds. They were honest, poor, hard-working people. The three Kings were next to come to the Christ Child. They were willing to sacrifice many things to search for Him. Through them the news of the Redeemer spread to the East.

Jesus taught the complete love of God and love of neighbor. He did this by word and example. After thirty years of hidden life, He began His public life of three years.

Jesus preached on the hillsides, in the Temple, and by the seaside. Very often His hearers were slow to understand. Sometimes they went away and followed Him no longer. He would tell His followers many stories, which were called *parables*. Each parable contained a lesson about His new law of love.

Christ did more than just tell us how to live. His whole life is an example of how we should know, love, and serve God. Since He was God, as well as man, He gave us wonderful examples of obedience and humility. The Bible says He went about "doing good." Can you not do this also?

In order to draw more souls to follow Him as the Son of God, Christ performed many acts which no other person could ever do by himself. Some of these acts were raising the dead to life, curing the deaf, dumb, blind, and lame. We call such acts which are above all earthly power to perform, *miracles*. These miracles proved that Christ has not only a human nature like us but that He has also a divine nature, that is, that He is God.

Christ healing the sick

4. Christ, the Giver of Supreme Gifts

Up to this time, you have read about the gifts that several nations have contributed to world civilization. But no nation ever gave the world such gifts as did the Son of God.

The gift of Himself. On Holy Thursday, Christ instituted a great Sacrament. He gave us His Sacred Body and Blood to help us every day of our lives. Every day Christ continues to perform this miracle at Holy Mass.

The gift of loving forgiveness. The gates of heaven had been closed because of Adam's sin. Christ came on earth to pay back the price for sin. He did this by His sufferings and death. He was put to death on the cross because He loved mankind.

This crucifixion was God's way of showing us love and forgiveness. Every crucifix is a story of the great love of God. You share in this forgiveness in a very special way when you go to confession. Do you thank God for this great gift of His love? By His own power, Christ rose from the

Jesus walked along this narrow street to Calvary

dead three days after dying on the cross. Forty days afterward, He ascended into heaven, again by His own power.

The gift of His grace. During Our Lord's public life, He appointed twelve helpers, called Apostles. These He instructed and taught His truths and doctrine, or teachings. He chose Peter to be their chief, and gave him the keys to the Kingdom of Heaven.

Our Lord knew His Apostles would need courage to preach and teach His word. Just before His Ascension, He told the Apostles to wait and pray in Jerusalem. They were to pray that the Holy Spirit would come to them. They did as they were commanded.

On the tenth day, the Holy Spirit brought them gifts of grace. They received all the grace they needed to do God's will.

You, too, have received the gift of God's holy grace. You became a child of God by grace in Baptism. At Confirmation you will receive still more grace. You have already learned about the gifts of Penance and Holy Eucharist. Can you name the other Sacraments which are God's gifts of grace?

Christ saves Saint Peter

5. Christ, the King

Very often Our Lord spoke about a Kingdom. He told many parables about the Kingdom of God. In the "Lord's Prayer," which is the *Our Father,* Christ taught the Apostles to say: "Thy Kingdom come."

Many Jewish people were jealous of Christ's power and influence. They were afraid Christ would become an earthly king. Herod was one of these jealous men. The chief men in the Jewish Court were jealous also.

But Christ's Kingdom was spiritual. The Kingdom of Christ on earth is His Mystical Body, the Church. Christ

JESUS DIES ON THE CROSS

God sent His Son, Jesus, to establish and prove the truth of His Church. To further give mankind the means of living their faith, Jesus gave them the seven Sacraments:

THE SACRAMENTS

1. Baptism. 2. Confirmation.
3. Holy Eucharist. 4. Penance.
5. Extreme Unction. 6. Holy Orders.
7. Matrimony.

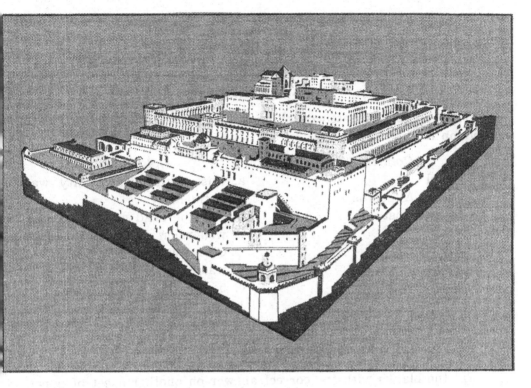

Solomon's Temple

taught us how to belong to His spiritual Kingdom. If we make use of the wonderful gifts He gives us, we shall have the peace of Christ in our souls. Later, Christ will come to take us to His eternal Kingdom in Heaven.

The Kingdom of God on earth has no boundary lines as earthly kingdoms have. It extends to all lands and all peoples. God creates the hearts and souls of all for His love and service. Those who are faithful to His spiritual Kingdom on earth will be taken later to the Kingdom of God in heaven.

The birth of Christ is the center of all civilization. When Christ came to the world, the greatest change came to civilization. The gates of heaven were opened by His death.

Christ taught the world a new law of love. The poor, the rich, the people made slaves by others, and the sickly were regarded by Him as equal. He taught that every human being has a right to be respected as a person. Christ raised womanhood to a higher place than it had before.

Words to Study

census   anointed spiritual aqueducts gladiators   Coliseum
doctrine parables miracles benefactor supernatural Mystical Body

Matching Exercise

Write complete sentences by matching correctly Column A with Column B.

Column A
1. David
2. Caesar Augustus
3. Jesus Christ
4. Mary
5. Joseph
6. St. Peter

Column B
a. was a king whose city was Bethlehem
b. was the head of the Apostles
c. was ruler of the world when Christ was born
d. was born in Bethlehem
e. became the Mother of God
f. traveled to Bethlehem with Mary

Completion Exercise

Fill the blanks with the correct answer on another sheet of paper. Select the correct answer from the words above.

1. spiritual
2. above all earthly power
3. B.C.
4. aqueducts
5. anointed
6. parables
7. Lord's Prayer
8. Holy Mass
9. Coliseum
10. miracles
11. Mystical Body
12. supernatural gifts

a. The _____ in Rome seated 80,000 people.
b. The abbreviation for "Before Christ" is _____.
c. The word "Christ" means ____ _____.
d. _____ were structures erected to bring water to Rome.
e. Christ founded a _____ kingdom in the souls of men.
f. _____ are deeds which are _____.

g. The great spiritual gifts God gave us are _____ _____.
h. The prayer taught us by Christ is the Our Father, also called the _____ _____.
i. Christ offers Himself for us at _____ every day.
j. The stories Our Lord told are called _____.
k. The Kingdom of Christ on earth is His _____.

CHAPTER II

ROME, THE CENTER OF CHRISTIANITY

The Church, God's gift. In the first chapter of this Unit, you studied about the birth of Christ. You learned about the wonderful gifts of God to mankind. No one but God could bestow such marvelous gifts on the world.

In order to help us get to heaven, Christ founded His Church. The birthday of the Catholic Church is Pentecost. On the first Pentecost the Holy Spirit came down upon the Apostles. That same Holy Spirit will stay with the Catholic Church until the end of time.

This chapter tells how the Catholic Church was established. It explains how the early Christians lived. It tells of the great work the Apostles did for the love of God.

1. Fearful Men Become Fearless

The first Pentecost. Before Christ ascended into heaven, He told the Apostles to return to Jerusalem to pray. They went to the Upper Room with our Blessed Mother. They were very much afraid that certain Jews would put them to death. We say they were fearful.

These Apostles did not yet understand all our Lord had said. They kept on praying, knowing that Christ would keep His promise. Christ promised to send them the Paraclete, that is, the Holy Spirit.

On the tenth day, the Holy Spirit came and descended upon them. He filled their souls with great courage. Now they were fearless. They understood all that God wanted them to do. They had been strengthened by the Holy Ghost. They went out to work, suffer, and die for Christ.

On that same day, Saint Peter preached his first sermon. Many people who heard him spoke other languages.

The first Pentecost

Yet everyone understood him in his own language. About three thousand people were converted that day.

This happened fifty days after Christ rose from the dead. The Greek word for "fifty" gives us the word Pentecost. This feast was the birthday of the Catholic Church.

Before our Lord ascended into heaven, He told His Apostles: "All power is mine in heaven and on earth. Go, therefore, teach all nations, baptizing them in the name of the Father, and of the Son, and of the Holy Spirit."

The Apostles began at once to obey Christ's command.

They preached in Palestine where Saint Peter remained for a time. Then each of the other Apostles went to different parts of the Roman Empire. Some went through Asia Minor, Syria, Russia, and Greece. Others went to Persia, India, and Africa.

First center of the Church. Many of the Jews were not eager to receive the teachings of the Apostles. Saint Peter left Jerusalem and traveled to Antioch (an'-tee-ok), the capital of Syria. Here he set up the first center of the Christian Church.

Many people thought the Christian religion was for the Jews only. But when Saint Peter came to Antioch, he received other people into the Church and baptized them. People who are not Jews are called gentiles. Now both Jews and gentiles were receiving the word of God. They were *followers of Christ,* so they were called *Christians.* It is important to remember that at Antioch, people were first called Christians.

Things that helped spread Christianity. God had planned that certain things already developed in civilization should help spread knowledge of His Law. First, there was a com-

JESUS GIVES ST. PETER THE KEYS

Many years after God gave mankind the Ten Commandments to teach them how to live, He sent His Son, Jesus, on earth to establish His Church and strengthen mankind by the sacraments to live the commandments and save their souls.

In giving the keys to Peter, Jesus said: "Thou art Peter, and upon this rock I will build my church." The signs that God founded the Church are these four marks:

THE MARKS OF THE CHURCH

1. One, because all its members profess the same faith, have the same sacrifice and sacraments, and are united under the Pope.
2. Holy, because it was founded by Christ, who is all holy, and because it teaches holy doctrines, provides the means of leading a holy life, and gives holy members to every age.
3. Catholic, because it will last for all time, and fulfills God's command to teach all nations the truths revealed by God.
4. Apostolic, because it was founded by Christ on the Apostles, and because, according to His divine will, it has always been governed by their lawful successors.

mon language. Most people in the Empire could speak Greek. It was easy, then, for the Apostles to be understood. Second, the fine Roman roads made it easy for the Apostles to travel. Third, the world was at peace. The Apostles could freely enter any land. This was the time in history called the "Roman Peace." These things were part of God's plan to help spread His Gospel.

The writers of the Gospels. The word "Gospel" means "good news." The story of Christ's life became known as the Gospel story. Now four men wrote the account of Christ's life, so there are four Gospels. Two of these men were Apostles, Matthew, and John. The other two Gospel writers were followers of Christ, called disciples. Their names were Mark and Luke. You hear a part of the Gospel read at Holy Mass. It comes from the writings of one of these four men. The four Gospels are in the Bible. They are in the part called the New Testament.

2. The Early Christian Church

The Apostles gave very careful instructions before they baptized their converts. They offered up the Holy Sacrifice of the Mass and administered the Sacraments.

The Apostles were just and charitable in governing their converts. They taught that all men are equal in the sight of God. They taught new lessons never before taught by any of the pagan religions. The poor were taught that they can share in the rewards of the Kingdom of Heaven as well as the rich. The Christian religion gave man great hope and dignity.

The Apostles ordain other priests. The Apostles knew that they could not rule all the communities alone. The Apostles ordained priests who celebrated Mass and administered most of the Sacraments. Some of these priests were consecrated bishops by the Apostles. The Apostles gave these bishops power to ordain and appoint others as they had done.

Still other helpers were needed for the Apostles. These helpers were called deacons. They distributed food, clothing, and other goods needed by the Christians in their daily life. One of these deacons was Saint Stephen. He became the first Christian to die for Christ. We celebrate his feast on December 26.

People became members of the Church through Baptism. They all believed the same truths and received the same Sacraments. They obeyed the bishop who was appointed to govern the Christians. The bishop had priests and deacons to help him.

Whenever the Apostles had to leave a city where they had taught the Christian religion, they left a bishop and priests in charge of the faithful Christians.

Life among the early Christians. The lives of the early Christians were very different from the lives of the pagans around them. At first they used to meet together in little groups like one large family. They practised true charity by sharing one another's goods.

The rich sold their property and gave the money to the Apostles. This money was for the good of everyone. All, rich and poor, freely and gladly gave their goods to be used by all for the love of Christ. They saw Christ in each other.

The early Christians shared their goods freely with one another. They acted purely from love of God. There is always peace and happiness in living according to God's Law.

This is the freedom we enjoy in our holy religion.

This is one reason why Christianity is so different from Communism. Communism does not teach love but hate. It makes men slaves of the state, not brothers in Christ. It forces men to give up things which really belong to them.

3. Saint Paul, Hater and Lover of Christ

Saul of Tarsus. Among the early converts to the Christian faith, the greatest was a man named Saul. Saul was a Jewish tentmaker who lived in Tarsus. Saul was brought up as a boy to hate the Christian religion. Later, he went from place to place arresting Christians.

When Saint Stephen, the deacon, was ordered to be stoned to death, Saul was present. He took part in this terrible deed by holding the coats of the men who stoned Stephen. Saint Stephen prayed for those who were putting him to death. God heard the prayers of Stephen.

A new convert. A short time later, Saul was traveling to the city of Damascus (da-mas'-kus). He was hunting for Christians. He had orders to arrest them when he reached the city. Suddenly a heavenly light blinded him and he fell down. At the same time, Saul heard a voice, saying, "Saul, Saul, why are you persecuting Me?" Saul asked, "Who art Thou, Lord?" The answer came, "I am Jesus, whom thou persecutest." Saul humbly asked, "Lord, what wilt Thou have me to do?"

Our Lord told him what to do. He went into the city, but he did not arrest any Christians. He was led through the streets of Damascus until he reached the home of a certain Christian. There he was baptized, and received the Holy Spirit. His name was changed from Saul to Paul. After this, his eyesight was restored.

Paul never did anything by halves. He could hate greatly, but he could love greatly, too. He hated Christ before his conversion. He was cruel to the Christians. Now he loved Christ so much that he spent the rest of his life preaching about the goodness of God. He brought many converts to the Christian Church.

Missions of Saint Paul. Paul began his preaching in Damascus. The Jews did not like this, so Paul went back to Jerusalem. It was very hard for the Christians there to believe that Paul

A Light from Heaven

was in earnest. They were afraid to trust him because he had had such a hatred of Christ in the past.

However, one man, named Barnabas, defended Saul. The Apostles then made Paul their friend. They gave Paul permission to preach in Jerusalem. Next Paul was sent to Tarsus, where he won many souls to Christ.

While Saint Peter was at Antioch, he sent for Saint Paul to come there to work with him. You will remember that it was here Saint Peter preached to the gentiles. Saint Paul made so many converts among the gentiles that he is called the "Apostle of the Gentiles."

For twenty years Paul traveled from place to place preaching the Gospel to the gentiles. Sometimes he traveled alone. At other times he traveled with a companion, such as his friend Timothy. He established small communities of Christians in Asia Minor. He traveled on foot all through Greece and Macedonia. He preached at Athens and Corinth. Paul could speak Greek very well, so the people understood him.

Whenever Saint Paul left a city, he put a bishop in charge. He liked to keep in touch with his people and came back to visit his converts when he could. Very often, he wrote letters to the bishop and people of the city. These letters were called Epistles (eh-pis'-uls). Two of these were to his companion, Saint Timothy.

Each Epistle began with a friendly greeting. Then it would remind the people that they were all called to be saints. Sometimes it would instruct them about their duties as Christians. Sometimes it would correct them for some evil thing they had done. Always it would show Saint Paul's great love for the people.

Other Apostles also wrote letters or Epistles. Portions of these Epistles are read at Holy Mass. They teach us how to live better lives as Catholics. We should read these Epistles. They can teach us many lessons.

While Saint Paul was going about from one place to another, Saint Peter was busy, too. He had left Antioch, and gone to Rome. There Saint Peter started the first Christian community in that city. Finally, Saint Paul came to Rome also, and preached the Word of God there with Saint Peter.

4. The Holy Spirit Guides the Church

Rome, you know, was the capital city of the world at that time. Saint Peter was the first Bishop of Rome. He was also the head of the entire Christian Church and the first Pope. Because he lived at Rome, that city became the chief center of the Christian religion.

All through the years, the Holy Spirit has guided the Church. The Church cannot make a mistake in its teachings because the Holy Spirit is with it always. So long as the world exists, Christ's Church will exist also.

Through the Holy Spirit the Church gives holiness to all its members. Because of this we say that when the Church speaks, God speaks. The Holy Spirit also helps the Church to protect the rights and gifts which God gave to man. One of these rights of man is the right to freedom.

The Church wants freedom to be used in the way God intended. Those who follow Christ and the teachings of His Church have freedom. Saint John calls this kind of freedom, the freedom of the sons of God.

New Words in This Chapter

Pentecost   Gospel   disciple   gentile   Christian   Epistle

A Test of Your Understanding

Do you understand what you have just read? If so, then you will receive a perfect score on this test. Number your paper 1 to 16, and write *Yes,* or *No,* after each.

1. Was the first center of the Church in Antioch?
2. Does the word "gentile" mean people who are not Jews?
3. Does the word Pentecost mean ten?
4. Is Pentecost the birthday of the Church?
5. Were the Apostles praying at Jerusalem when the Holy Spirit came?
6. Were the early Christians forced to give up their property?
7. Did Saint Paul preach in Athens?
8. Did all Christians trust Paul after his conversion?
9. Was Saint Paul the first Pope?
10. Did Rome later become the center of the Christian religion under Peter?

Matching Words with Their Meanings

Match these two columns on your paper. Write in complete sentences.

Column A	*Column B*
1. Deacons	a. were people who were not Jews
2. Disciples	b. were those who were followers of Christ
3. Christians	c. were the closest friends of our Lord
4. Apostles	d. were men who followed our Lord also

5. Gentiles   e. were men who helped the Apostles to do acts of charity

Review of Unit Three

Important facts in this Unit are:

1. Christ came to found a Kingdom that would last forever in Heaven.
2. The birth of Christ is the turning-point of human history.
3. Christ's birth marks the beginning of a great change in civilization.
4. Christ taught man a new law of love.
5. Christ gave the world greater gifts than any one else could bestow on the world.
6. Christ redeemed the world by His death on the cross. Only God could make up for Adam's sin.
7. Christ founded His Church to bring all men the help they need to save their souls.
8. Antioch was the first center of the Christian Church.
9. Greek language, Roman roads, and Roman peace helped spread the true religion.
10. Saint Paul was a convert who became the greatest Apostle of the Gentiles.
11. Man may not be forced to give up his property. Man may share his property with others, if he desires to do so, for the love of Christ.
12. Rome became the center of the Christian religion under Saint Peter, the first Pope.
13. God planned that the civilization of the Roman Empire would help spread the teachings of Christianity.
14. The Holy Ghost is the guide of the Church. The Holy Spirit will not let the Church make a mistake. The Holy Spirit will remain with the Church until time is no more.

Something to Help You Learn

1. Make a booklet on "The Lord's Prayer." Find pictures about the different parts of the Our Father. Paste them in your booklet and write underneath the words which the pictures represent.
2. Find out what figures represent the four writers of the Gospel. Your teacher will help you to locate these four symbols.
3. Write a play on the way the early Christians lived. Make it very simple, with only two or three persons talking. Make it very brief.
4. Pretend you were in Athens when Saint Paul was preaching. Write down four sen-

tences which you think he would have said.

5. Make a booklet on the "Early Christian Church." Tell the story of Saint Stephen and Saint Paul's conversion.
6. Draw an outline map of the Old World; write Antioch, Rome, Athens, and Corinth in the proper places.
7. Find pictures on the Life of our Lord, and paste them in your scrapbook. You may do the same with the mysteries of the Rosary.

Mastery Test

I. On another sheet of paper copy these sentences, filling in the correct answer from the terms in the parenthesis.

1. Christ was born in (Bethlehem, Rome, Nazareth, Antioch).
2. The birthday of the Church is (Christmas, Easter, Pentecost, All Saints Day).
3. We learn about the life of Christ from (Roman law, Gospels, Greek thinkers, Caesar).
4. Christ chose (nine, four, twelve, seven) Apostles.
5. Christ told His Apostles to teach (wealthy people, Jewish people, Romans, all nations).
6. Saint Peter was Bishop of (Athens, Jerusalem, Corinth, Rome).
7. Saint Paul was converted on his way to (Rome, Antioch, Damascus, Tarsus).
8. The letters Saint Paul wrote are called (Gospels, Epistles, literature, poetry).
9. Saint Stephen was the first Christian who was (converted, martyred, baptized, arrested).
10. The first Emperor of Rome was (Caesar, Saint Peter, David, Caesar Augustus).

II. Place these events in the order in which they happened. Rearrange them correctly on your paper.

1. Death of Christ
2. Conversion of St. Paul
3. Birth of Christ
4. Resurrection from the dead of our Lord
5. Pentecost

III. Arrange these events in the order in which they happened.

1. Antioch became the center of Christianity
2. Rome became the center of Christianity

3. Caesar Augustus called for a census
4. Christ's death on the cross
5. Pentecost

IV. Answer the following on your paper.

1. Is the Pope the visible Head of the Church or is Christ the visible Head?
2. To what city was Saul going to arrest the Christians?
3. How did Saint Paul keep in touch with his converts in different places?
4. Which two Apostles wrote Gospels?
5. What do the Letters "A.D." mean?
6. Who was Emperor during the "Golden Age of Rome"?
7. What were Rome's two greatest contributions to civilization?
8. Is Rome the center of Christianity today?
9. How did Romans celebrate the victory of a great general?
10. Who told the Apostles that Saint Paul was a true convert?

V. Fill in the blanks in the following exercise.

1. Followers of Christ are called _____.
2. Saint Timothy was a companion of Saint _____.
3. Two Greek cities where Saint Paul preached are _____ and _____.
4. Two disciples who wrote Gospels but were not Apostles were _____ and _____.
5. While Saint _____ was being slain, Saul _____.
6. A portion of one of the _____ and one of the _____ is read at Mass.

VI. Answer the following in full sentences.

1. How is the Church still following God's command to teach all nations?
2. Why is the birth of Christ the greatest event in all history?
3. Why do we say that Christ changed the civilization in the world?
4. Tell three things that helped carry out God's plan for the world's redemption.
5. Tell what is meant by Christ's new law of love.

Hymns to Mary

HISTORY OF HYMNS. In 596 an epidemic was raging in Rome. Pope St. Gregory the Great ordered a procession to pray to God that the epidemic might cease. As the people passed the tomb of Hadrian on the Tiber River, the voices of angels were heard in the heavens. The angels sang "Queen of Heaven, rejoice, alleluia . . ." Pope Gregory added, "Pray for us to God, alleluia." As a result of these prayers, the epidemic stopped. The hymn, "Queen of Heaven, Rejoice" is still sung during Easter time.

ORIGIN AND MEANING. The *Stabat Mater* was written in Latin in the 14th century. It is thought that the author was Jacopone de Todi, a Franciscan friar. During the Middle Ages the *Stabat Mater* was often sung during processions honoring the Passion of our Lord. We usually sing it now during the Stations of the Cross. The *Stabat Mater* has been translated into English by many writers, about 65 in all. The translation which is most famous is that of Father Edward Caswall.

Stabat Mater

At the Cross her station keeping,
Stood the mournful Mother weeping,
Close to Jesus to the last.

Through her heart, His sorrow sharing,
All His bitter anguish bearing,
Now at length the sword had passed.

Oh, how sad and sore distressed
Was that Mother highly blessed
Of the sole-begotten One!

Christ above in torment hangs,
She beneath beholds the pangs
Of her dying, glorious Son.

Is there one who would not weep
Whelmed in miseries so deep
Christ's dear Mother to behold?

Can the human heart refrain
From partaking in her pain
In that Mother's pain untold?

Bruised, derided, cursed, defiled,
She beheld her tender child,
All with bloody scourges rent.

APPLICATION. Mary, the Mother of Sorrows, lived to see her Son, Jesus, die on the Cross. Sorrow, like a sword, pierced her heart, as the prophet Simeon had foretold.
We run into many occasions of sorrow and regrets. It requires fortitude and faith to face the future. Mary was able to overcome the greatest of all sorrows.

Courtesy of Rev. J. B. Carol, O. F. M.

UNIT FOUR

CHRISTIAN CIVILIZATION IS CHALLENGED

UNIT FOUR

CHRISTIAN CIVILIZATION IS CHALLENGED

Do you know what a challenge is? It is a call to take part in a contest of some kind. To challenge also means to question the truth of what someone believes. It means that one is put to a test or time of trial.

This is what happened to Christian civilization. It was tested in three ways. The struggle was a long one. It continued for many years. Christian civilization suffered from the Emperors, from people outside the Empire, and from enemies of the Church.

When Saint Peter first went to Rome, the Christians were very few. At first the Roman Emperor did not notice that the Christian religion was growing. But when some enemies of Christ informed him

about it he became alarmed. He tried to do away with this new religion.

Nero and several Emperors after him made the Christians suffer and die for their religion. The Christians gladly suffered everything, even death, for the sake of Jesus Christ. In one way the persecution, or sufferings of the Christians, brought the Christians closer together.

For three hundred years these persecutions went on. Then religious freedom was granted to all within the Empire. This freedom was granted by an Emperor named Constantine. This Unit Four will tell us about him and how the condition of the Christians was improved by this Roman Emperor.

CHAPTER I

THE CHRISTIANS SUFFER BUT CONQUER

Points to remember. Rome, the great city of the Emperors, became the center of the Christian religion. It was in this city that Saint Peter dwelt. Saint Paul, too, came to work for souls in Rome.

But things did not go along so smoothly for the Christians in Rome. Many of them had to give up their lives for the sake of their faith. But this does not mean that the Christians did not obtain new converts. It was just the other way around. The Christians became more and more numerous, even though so many of them were being slain, or put to death. God planned it that way. No matter what happens, the Catholic Church will not disappear from the world. It will last forever.

In this chapter you will learn about the many sufferings of the early Christians and what happened to relieve their troubles.

1. The Emperor Nero

During the reign of the Roman Emperor, Nero, a great fire broke out in the city of Rome. Many people who did not like the Christians blamed them for this fire.

The Emperor Nero began to persecute the Christians. He did everything he could to cause them great suffering. He put many of them to death.

Our Lord had told His followers that they would suffer for His sake. Those who died for Him are called *martyrs* (mar'-ters). This word means "witness." All the martyrs were witnesses for Christ.

Death of Saints Peter and Paul. It was during this persecution that Saints Peter and Paul were martyred. Saint Peter was crucified with his head down. Saint Paul was a Roman citizen. It was against the law for a Roman citizen to be crucified. So Saint Paul was beheaded.

Every one of the Apostles, except Saint John, was put to death for preaching about Christ. Saint John was put into a large cauldron, or tub, of boiling oil. He walked out of it unhurt. He was the only Apostle to die a natural death.

The Church did not die with the martyrdom of Saint Peter and the other Apostles. The other followers of Christ carried on the great work in the Church. Christ, the invisible Head, continued to protect and guide the Church throughout the years. Christ is still with His Church today.

Culver Service
The angel frees Saint Peter from prison

2. Other Persecutions

The Christians obeyed the laws of the Romans. They paid their taxes, prayed for the Emperor, and even fought in his wars. They taught their children love for parents and respect for womanhood.

The Christians gave up old pagan customs when they became converts. They were forbidden to attend pagan plays. They were forbidden to marry anyone except a fellow Christian. They were forbidden to offer incense to the pagan gods. The Christians believed that the true God is greater than any government or emperor or state. This made the Romans angry. They called the Christians traitors. Often they blamed the Christians for crimes which, of course, they did not commit.

Sufferings of the Christians. The Romans punished cruelly those who would not worship false gods. Sometimes the Emperor was regarded as a god. But the Christians would not worship him.

Thousands of Christians were thrown into prison. Others were tossed to the wild beasts for the entertainment of the pagans. Some were covered with tar and burned as torches.

The Coliseum where many Christians were put to death

The Christians chose suffering and death rather than deny Christ. Some of them even begged to die as martyrs. Saint Lawrence, a deacon, was burned to death on a gridiron. In the midst of his sufferings, he said to his torturers, "Turn me over, for I think I am done on that side."

Christian heroes and heroines. Even boys and girls were among the martyrs. Saint Agnes was only twelve years old. No matter how the pagan men tried to scare her, she would not give up her holy religion. The Romans were so angry that they finally cut off her head. Saint Agnes is a model for a pure and holy life.

The young boy, Tarcisius (tar-see'-see-us) was a very brave Christian. During the persecutions, the priests could not visit the prisons. Therefore the Christians could not receive Holy Communion. As Tarcisius was only a boy, the guards often let him visit the prison.

The priests knew this, so they allowed Tarcisius to bring Holy Communion to the Christians. None of the guards ever knew what Tarcisius was doing.

One day, on his way to prison, some rough boys trapped Tarcisius. They tried to make him give up whatever he was carrying. Tarcisius firmly refused to let the Blessed Sacrament out of his hands. The boys then beat him to death. Even then they could not take the Blessed Sacrament away from him. This was a miracle which God was pleased to allow for His greater glory.

A brave Roman soldier named Sebastian (se-bas'-chan) was pierced with arrows. He was then left to die, tied to a tree. But he did not die, so he was afterwards put to death by the sword.

Length of the persecutions. The persecutions lasted during the reigns of several Emperors. There were about ten persecutions in all. One of the worst persecutions was that by the Emperor Diocletian (die-owe-clee'-shan). He thought he could make his empire strong by wiping out Christianity.

3. The Church Saved in the Catacombs

Burial of the Christians. The

Philip Gendreau, N. Y.
Mass in a Roman catacomb

early Christians showed great respect for the bodies of their martyrs. They buried them in long underground tunnels dug out of soft rock. These run for about seven hundred miles underneath Rome and outside it. The tunnels or caves are called catacombs.

In these catacombs the Christians hollowed out spaces in the walls. Here they made the tombs and covered them with marble slabs. These slabs were beautifully decorated with pictures of our Lord, His Blessed Mother, or some other painting about religion.

Holy Mass in the catacombs. The Christians met for Mass in lit-

Inside one of the catacombs

tle chapels in the catacombs. They began to use the tomb of a martyr for an altar. From the Mass and the Sacraments they gained strength to live and die for Christ. Our religion has not changed. We, too, get grace and strength from attending Holy Mass and receiving the Sacraments. This is so even if we are in a fine church and in no danger from enemies.

Just as in the early days, every priest now says Mass on an altar stone. This stone contains a relic, or part of the body, of a martyr or a saint.

4. Christianity, the Religion of the Empire

The Emperors give up. After the terrible persecution of Diocletian, something happened to end the persecutions of the Christians. A man named Constantine (kon'-stan-tine) became Emperor. He treated the Christians very differently from earlier Emperors.

The True Cross is found. Constantine was not a Christian but his mother was a very fervent one. Her name was Helena. She wanted very much to find the cross upon which our Lord died. When she **was**

very old, she made a long journey to Jerusalem to search for the sacred relic. After some time, she found three crosses. One of these she knew, must be the cross upon which Christ had been crucified. A woman who had for a long time been ill, was brought to Saint Helena. Saint Helena had the woman touched with the crosses, one at a time. When the woman was touched by the third cross, she was instantly cured of her illness. Saint Helena knew that this was God's way of pointing out to her the True Cross. In the following paragraphs you shall discover what the cross meant to Saint Helena's son, the Emperor.

A sign to Constantine. Constantine had some enemies among the Romans. They went to battle against him. On the night before the great battle Constantine had a dream. He saw a cross in the sky with the words, "In this sign thou shalt conquer" written around it. This dream made Constantine change his banner before going to battle. He took the Roman eagle from his banner and put in its place the form of the cross.

Constantine rode forth at the

Culver Service
Constantine

head of his soldiers. He came back from battle as the winner. He made it plain to everyone that the God of the Christians had won the battle for him.

Command of Constantine. At once Constantine wrote an order for his Empire. He wrote: "We grant to the Christians and to all others the freedom to follow the way of worship which they may choose." This order is very important. It is called the Edict of Milan. This edict gave Christians the freedom they wanted and to which they had a right. It happened in the year 313 A.D.

Constantine gave the Chris-

Screen Traveler, from Gendreau

The Arch of Constantine in Rome. Why did the Romans build such arches?

tians the right to own property again. All that had been taken away from them was returned. He allowed the churches to be opened again.

Constantine himself did not become a Christian until shortly before his death.

Paganism on the way out. After 313 A.D. the Christians were no longer persecuted. But the pagans still had their temples to their gods after that. They still held festivals in honor of their pagan gods, too.

By 395 A.D. a Catholic Emperor came to the throne of the Roman Empire. His name was Theodosius (the-owe-doe'-shi-us). He made Christianity *the* religion of the Empire. He closed all the pagan temples and would not allow any pagan ceremonies in Rome at all. Theodosius wanted all the Romans to be Christians.

God is the Founder of the true religion. The teachings of Christianity led to a better way of living in the world. Christianity also saved the best of ancient civilization from being destroyed. The world still benefits from this.

Do You Know the Meaning of These Words?

edict	martyr	catacomb	paganism
convert	relic	persecution	ceremonies

Discussion Topics

1. What does the altar stone remind you of?
2. Why did the early Christians build catacombs?

3. Is the Mass said in your church today as good for your soul as the Mass said in the catacombs?

Test Yourself

Select the correct answer from each number below and write that letter on your paper.

1. The apostles proved that what they taught was true by (a) traveling, (b) giving goods away, (c) performing miracles, (d) playing games.
2. The Christians held secret meetings in (a) temples, (b) forum, (c) catacombs, (d) Coliseum.
3. The altar stone reminds us of (a) the Rock of Saint Peter, (b) the Last Supper, (c) the catacombs, (d) Rosetta Stone.
4. A martyr means (a) saying many prayers, (b) being a witness for Christ, (c) being kind to everyone, (d) being a traitor to Christ.
5. The saint who found the True Cross was (a) Saint Sebastian, (b) Saint Agnes, (c) Saint Lawrence, (d) Saint Helena.
6. A relic is (a) something stolen, (b) something belonging to a saint, (c) part of a stone in the catacombs, (d) a prayer said at Mass.
7. The Emperor who made Christianity the religion of the Empire was (a) Constantine, (b) Nero, (c) Diocletian, (d) Theodosius.
8. Saint Paul was martyred by (a) crucifixion, (b) being burned alive, (c) the sword, (d) being thrown to wild beasts.
9. The persecutions lasted from the time of Nero to (a) Theodosius, (b) Constantine, (c) Diocletian, (d) Saint Lawrence.
10. The saint crucified with head down was (a) Lawrence, (b) Sebastian, (c) Peter, (d) Tarcisius.

CHAPTER II

STRANGERS TAKE OVER THE EMPIRE

For about two hundred years after the death of Augustus, the government went along as usual. Augustus' plan of government was so great that it was followed even after his death. The Emperors were not always good leaders. Some were bad, indeed. But, for the most part, the Roman government continued to work.

Little by little, a great change came over the Roman Empire. It was a very trying time for Rome and the whole of civilization. There were many evils growing within the Empire itself. These evils made Rome a weak nation. Evil always is a sign of weakness.

Besides the evil within, there were foes outside the Empire. They lived north of the Rhine River. As Rome grew weaker and weaker, the enemies of Rome became stronger. At last the time came when these strangers came right into the Empire. They made their homes there and took full charge of the government.

1. Evils within the Empire

Emperors from the army. As the Roman people became weaker, the army became stronger. That meant that the army chose the Emperor it wanted. There was no way of knowing who would be the next Emperor. Sometimes different generals would fight for the throne. The winner would then take over the Empire and rule it.

Such a thing was not good for Rome. Sometimes these Emperors were able to rule wisely and well. Always, however, it was hard for any man to control such a large Empire by himself.

This was going on when the Christians were being persecuted. These Emperors chosen from the army were called "Barrack Emperors."

Other men fight for Rome. In the early days of Rome, the people were patriotic. But as more and more Greek slaves began to teach Roman boys, Romans began to lose their patriotism. When these boys were older, they had no desire to fight for Rome. They had no love for their country. Besides they did not want to work hard for anything but pleasure.

So it came about that men from other lands were hired to fight in Rome's army. These hired soldiers came from lands north of Italy. They were called *Germans* or *Teutons* (tue′-tons). These men had no love for Rome. They fought only for the salary they received. This was another evil that made the Empire weak.

The Germans were not civilized like the Romans. They did not have the culture or training of the Romans. For this reason they are called *barbarians*. However, while they were in the army, they mixed with Roman soldiers.

From them they learned many Roman ways of doing things. In turn, they taught the Romans some good and bad habits of life. We say that they blended their customs and culture into a *new way of living*. You will read more about this later.

Romans lead bad lives. The Romans led bad lives during these pagan days. They spent most of their time attending games, going to banquets, and watching entertainments. They left all their work to their slaves. As a result of this, they lost their own strength through lack of exercise.

These were not the worst evils of the Romans. Worst of all, they satisfied every wish and desire of their bodies. They committed many crimes, such as divorce and murder of the young and innocent and thought only of themselves.

No money in Rome. There were no longer many wealthy noble families in Rome. The citizens did not pay taxes. There was no way of forcing them to pay. Some of them had wasted all their money and could not pay taxes at any rate. Others were out of work and this made them penniless.

The provinces were taxed more and more. But these people were no better off than the Romans themselves. They could not afford to pay taxes either.

Everything in decay and ruin. Trade within the Empire died out slowly. No one could buy any goods. There were no jobs for people to earn money. Just imagine what would happen if no one in your town or city had a chance to earn a living. Everything would be left without care or attention. Diseases would break out and food would be scarce. We have had "hard times" in our country in the past. People still talk of the days of the "depression." But such "hard times" in our country were never as bad as in Rome.

2. A New Capital Is Built

Trouble ahead for the Empire. During these days of unrest the Emperors had other serious troubles. From time to time the large groups of people outside the Empire grew restless, too. They often tried to enter the Empire. The Emperors fought and fought to keep them out. They did cast them off in the beginning. Besides this, Persia in the East was ready for war.

Plan of an Emperor. When Constantine became Emperor, he saw very well the great troubles of the Empire. He did all he could to strengthen Roman power.

Rome, you know, is in the center of Italy. The Germans were on the border of Italy. Rome was very far from the border. It was yet farther from the danger spots in the East.

Constantine did something no Emperor had ever done before. He built a new capital in the East. He chose the city of Byzantium (bi-zan'-shi-um) because it was near the Eastern border and could be protected too. Byzantium is on the banks of a narrow strip of water called the Strait of Bosporus. You will find it on your map between the Black Sea and the Mediterranean.

Constantine changed the name of the city from Byzantium to Constantinople. This name means "the City of Constantine."

The Empire is divided. Even before Constantine, some Emperors saw that it was impossible to rule the large Empire. They divided the land into sections. They gave certain trusted men charge of each section. But when some Emperors came into power, they would keep all power for themselves and try to rule alone.

After the time of Constantine, the Empire was divided into two parts, the Eastern and the Western Empire. Often the

Philip Gendreau, N. Y.

A view of modern Istanbul, the city once called Constantinople

Eastern Empire was called the Greek Empire. It became closely connected with Eastern ways of living and Greek culture. The famous capital of the Eastern Empire, of course, was Constantinople.

3. A Famous Eastern Emperor

One of the Emperors of the Eastern Empire was named Justinian (jus-tin'-ee-an). He was very successful in the wars which he carried on against the barbarians.

Work of Justinian. The greatest work of Justianian was that of collecting and arranging the laws. He gathered up all the laws of the Romans from the earliest days. Then he had them published under the name of the *Justinian Code*. Sometimes the collection is known as the "Body of Civil Law." This was a very important thing for the Eastern Empire and for the whole world after that. Lawmakers made a careful study of the Justinian Code. They based their new laws on what they discovered in the Body of Civil Law.

The church built by Justinian.

Justinian built a very beautiful church at Constantinople. This church was not built like the Roman churches. Instead, it was made like the Eastern buildings of that time. It had several small parts with domes covering them. In the center there was a large hall, also covered with a dome. The name of the church is "Sancta Sophia," which means *holy wisdom*. It was not named after a saint. It was named after our Lord, who is called the "Wisdom of God."

Sancta Sophia was made in the Eastern style of building, called Byzantine (biz-ant'-in) architecture. The customs and culture of the East are called Byzantine.

4. The Western Empire Falls to Pieces

You have seen that terrible evils had come upon the once mighty Roman Empire. These evils were not all from without. The worst evils of Rome came from within. The government was upset, the people had no work or money. Many of them were not leading good lives. All these things made Rome a weak nation.

Finally the time came when Rome was attacked from without. The barbarians were causing more and more trouble. Of course, there were many barbarians now getting along well in the Roman army. The longer they stayed in the army, the more they learned about the ways of civilization.

The fiercest of all. North of Rome, but away toward the East, lived the most savage of the barbarians. These fierce people were known as the Huns. Suddenly they dashed across Europe on their swift horses. They destroyed everything in their path. They were most cruel to those whom they conquered. Their savage deeds made everyone very much afraid of them.

The Teutons in the North. You have read earlier in this chapter about the barbarians who lived on the borderlands of Rome, beyond the Rhine River. Some of these had fought in Rome's army.

These Teutons, or Germans, were lovers of freedom. They lived as nomads, ever moving on in search of new or better hunting grounds. In many ways the Teutons lived as the Indians did in America before Columbus came.

The Teutons were divided into many tribes. When you are older you will read about

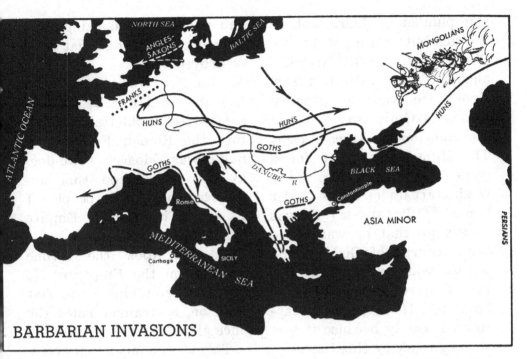

BARBARIAN INVASIONS

the Goths, Visigoths, Vandals, Franks, and Gauls or Celts. These were all members of the tribes known as Teutons.

The Goths help to crush the Huns. Rome was very much afraid of the Huns. The army was now very weak. So Rome asked the Goths to help fight the Huns. These people promised to do so if they could make their homes in the Empire as peaceful settlers. The Romans agreed to this.

Rome breaks a promise. Rome was saved from the Huns that time and all went well. However, the Goths did not get fair treatment from the Romans. Often the Gothic children were taken as slaves. The Romans cheated them in many ways.

This made the Goths very angry. A strong leader arose among them named Alaric (al'-a-rick). In 410 A.D. he attacked Rome. The city fell after six days of continual battle.

Stolen gifts and treasures. Not only were the great buildings of Rome destroyed. The Goths marched out of Rome laden with treasures untold. They took wagonloads of valuable jewels, gold, and works of art. Thousands of Romans were taken captive.

The Goths took great delight in destroying things. The "work of centuries" was stolen and plundered. Alaric robbed the rich but he did not destroy Christian churches. Alaric died along the way southward from Rome. He was the greatest leader the Goths ever had.

The Huns on the warpath again. The Huns were quiet for a while. Then they received a fresh start under a new leader named Attila (at'-i-la). He was so savage that he was called the "Scourge of God." Attila led his warriors into the Roman Empire. He had his eyes on Rome. He could have captured it easily because it was so very weak by this time.

The Pope, the Bishop of Rome, at that time was Leo, now called Saint Leo the Great. Pope Leo himself went to the camp of Attila. He asked him not to attack Rome. Attila admired the great courage and dignity of Pope Leo. As a result of this visit, Rome was saved. Attila told his soldiers to leave Rome immediately. After that, the Huns never threatened Rome again.

But the days of warfare were not over for Rome. For two hundred years other barbarian armies burned, robbed, killed, and made people captives. The Roman Empire was overrun by invaders. Everything was in ruins. Nothing was being done to replace the things that were destroyed.

An Empire crumbles to ruin. One day in 476 A.D. a handsome German chieftain walked into the Roman Forum. His name was Odoacer (owe-doe-ay'-ser). He made this announcement to the people of Rome: "The Roman Empire exists no longer."

Odoacer took the throne away from the Emperor. No one dared stop him. From that time on, a stranger ruled the once glorious city.

This was an important event. The Roman Empire had fallen. But it is also important to remember that it did not fall suddenly. It weakened slowly by evil from within before it was conquered by foes outside.

The Eastern Empire carries on. Only the Western Empire fell at this time. The Eastern Empire lasted for a thousand years afterward. Not until 1453 did the city of Constantinople fall into other hands.

Teutons and Romans live together. After the fall of Rome, the Teutons and Romans lived very closely together. By degrees these Teutons became more civilized. Out of this mixing or blending of Roman and

Teuton civilization came a new way of living. This new way of living was saved and guarded by the teachings of the Catholic Church. Through the Teutons Christian civilization spread to more peoples and nations.

A forward and backward look. The great work of Christian civilization met challenge. People from the north forced their way into Roman provinces. Some of them received their pay from the Roman army. These strangers were not so civilized as the Romans. They destroyed the treasures of civilization in many cities. They destroyed even Rome itself. This Unit shows that the Catholic Church was the one hope of the world at that time. The Church saved civilization and converted the barbarians. The fall of Rome meant that strangers took over the Empire.

The Catholic Church, too, was attacked and challenged. Some people began to spread false stories about it. Some began to teach *heresy,* or false doctrine. The Church did something about this. She assembled all the bishops together and held a Council, or meeting. At the first meeting, the bishops explained very clearly just what Christians believe and teach about Christ. The first general Council was held in 325 A.D.

We shall read about some of the great men of the Church. These gave their time, talents, and labor to the work of defending the Church against heresy. Their writings still exist and are still used to defend the Church. The greatest of these early Christian writers was the scholar, bishop, and monk, named Saint Augustine.

We shall find out that this man was very important. He was one of the greatest Doctors of the Church and one of the great men of history.

Word Study

barbarians	scourge
savage	architecture
blending	depression
code	dome
nomads	

Points to Talk About

1. How did Rome become so weak?
2. Why did Constantine move his capital to the East?
3. How did it happen that the Teutons were allowed to live in the Empire?
4. Why is the Emperor Justinian famous?

How Well Do You Remember?

Number a paper from 1 to 10. After each number write the words from the list preceding the exercise which will correctly fill the blanks.

Huns Attila Alaric Church Roman Empire Goths Pope Leo the Great

1. The ———— helped Rome defeat the other barbarians.
2. ———— was leader of the Goths.
3. ———— was leader of the Huns.
4. The ———— teaches all nations.
5. The most fierce of all barbarians were the ————.
6. In 476 A.D. the ———— fell.
7. Rome was saved because of ————.
8. The ———— was taken over by Odoacer.
9. ———— destroyed the great treasures of Rome.
10. Pope Leo the Great met ————, and asked him to spare Rome.

Can You Answer These Questions?

Write "Yes" or "No" after each of the following.

1. Did the army choose the Emperors in the early days?
2. Were the Huns part of the Teuton tribe?
3. Was Odoacer a Goth?
4. Is Byzantine culture that of the East?
5. Did Justinian write a code of laws?
6. Did Alaric steal treasures from Rome?
7. Was Justinian an Emperor of the Western Empire?
8. Did Pope Leo save the city of Constantinople?
9. Is Rome on the Strait of Bosporus?
10. Did Rome decay within before it fell to an outside enemy?
11. Is Byzantium the old name for Constantinople?
12. Was Alaric called "Scourge of God"?
13. Did the church of Sancta Sophia have Roman style of architecture?
14. Did the Teutons become members of the Roman army?

CHAPTER III

CHRISTIAN WRITERS DEFEND THE CHURCH

A glance ahead. In Unit Three we learned that Saint Paul wrote many Epistles to his new converts. Other Apostles wrote Epistles also.

The Apostles spent much of their time preaching the word of God to many nations. However, the four Gospels give us a written account of the life of Christ and His teachings. Those who wrote the Gospels are called *Evangelists* (e-van'-jel-ists). The disciple Saint Luke also wrote about the early Church and some of the travels of Saint Paul. We call this account the *Acts of the Apostles.*

In this chapter you will discover how the Church was guided after the death of the Apostles and those who knew Our Lord during His life. You will learn about saintly men whose writings, many explaining doctrine, are still important in the Church today.

1. Fathers of the Church

The pagans did not wipe out Christianity by persecuting the Christians. Instead, the Church grew stronger and stronger. Some people attacked the Church in another way. They spread stories about the Church that were not true so as to harm her.

God gave His Church holy men who defended the Church against these false stories. They wrote letters which helped the Church very much. Even today these letters give us much information about what the early Christians believed. The writers of the first centuries are called *Fathers of the Church.*

A pupil of Saint Peter. One of Saint Peter's pupils was named Ignatius (ig-nay'-shus). Saint Peter trusted him very much and made him Bishop of Antioch. Can you recall any important event connected with that

Culver Service

Saint Ignatius

map? Polycarp had been a pupil of Saint John the Apostle. He had many friends who had known and seen Christ. He was condemned to be burned to death because of his preaching. But his body would not burn. They had to kill him with a dagger.

Writer on the Holy Eucharist. One of the most powerful among the Fathers of the Church was one named Saint Irenaeus (i-re-nay'-us). This saint was trained by Saint Polycarp. He is remembered especially for his writings on the Holy Eucharist.

Saint Clement and Saint Justin were early writers also. All these early writers were called "Fathers of the Church" because of the importance of their writings on our holy faith.

2. The Creed Said at Mass

The creed which you know so well is called the Apostles' Creed. But when the priest says Mass on Sundays and some feast days, he uses a different Creed. It means the same as the Apostles' Creed but it is expressed in different words. Most of it was written at a place called Nicaea (nye-see'-a) in Asia Minor in 325

place? Saint Ignatius learned from the Apostles how to explain the teachings of Christ. He is called an Apostolic Father besides Father of the Church.

Now the pagans did not like Saint Ignatius. He would not let his Christians worship the Roman gods or the Emperor. As a punishment Ignatius was brought to Rome. He was thrown to the lions in the arena. Saint Ignatius was glad to be able to die for Christ.

A pupil of Saint John. Another early writer was Polycarp (pol'-i-karp), Bishop of Smyrna (smur'-na). Can you find that on your classroom

Culver Service

Saint Irenaeus

false doctrine. He is one of the Doctors of the Church. The word "doctor" means "teacher."

3. The First Latin Bible

Some parts of the Bible were written in Hebrew, some in the language called Aramaic, and some in Greek. Later, the Old Testament was translated into Greek. There were also some Latin translations of the Old Testament as well as the New. Latin, you know, became the common language of the Roman Empire.

Some of these Latin translations were not satisfactory, so the Pope asked that a new Latin translation be made.

A.D. That is why it was called the Nicene (nye-seen') Creed.

The Nicene Creed was written at the first big Council, or meeting, of the bishops of the Church. This Council had been called because some men were teaching that Jesus was not really God. At the Council the bishops wanted to be sure that everyone believed and taught the truth. They wrote the chief truths in the Nicene Creed.

A holy man. At this meeting there was a very holy person named Athanasius (a-tha-nay'-shus). He was a deacon who came from Alexandria with his bishop. Saint Athanasius fought very hard against this

Saint Athanasius

Culver Service

Culver Service

Saint Jerome

To translate anything into another language means a great deal of time and work. To translate the Bible, then, was a very great task. There lived in the early days a very holy man named Jerome. The Pope asked Saint Jerome to make a new Latin Bible. Saint Jerome worked hard on this great task. This Latin Bible is called the *Vulgate* (vul'-gate). This translation made by Saint Jerome is still used.

Saint Jerome is one of the Doctors of the Church. He well deserves this honor because of his many writings on Christian truth and teaching.

4. The Bishop of Milan

Saint Ambrose was the Bishop of Milan, a city in northern Italy. He is a very famous Doctor of the Church. Saint Ambrose did not fear to correct people when they were doing wrong. Once he went to the Emperor and scolded him for a great evil he had done. He made the Emperor do public penance for his sin and the scandal he caused. The Emperor obeyed Saint Ambrose, his bishop.

It was good for the people to see their Emperor obeying the Bishop. Many of the pagans had looked upon the Emperor as a god. Now they saw that he was human and weak and sometimes fell into sin.

When the Council of Nicaea met, they condemned a false teaching, called a *heresy*. This heresy was started by Arius, and was called Arianism. It taught that Jesus is not God. In the Western Church the bravest and strongest one to fight against this heresy was the Bishop of Milan, Saint Ambrose. While Saint Athanasius was fighting Arianism in the Eastern Church, Saint Ambrose was fighting it in the Western Church.

5. The Great Saint Augustine

The greatest of the Fathers of the Church is Saint Augustine. As wonderful as the others are, he is like a giant compared with them.

Early life. Saint Augustine was born in Africa. His father was a pagan, but his mother was a Christian. His mother, Monica, trained him in Christianity, but his father would not let him be baptized. When Augustine grew older he was sent to Carthage where he studied to become a teacher.

While Augustine was away at school in Carthage, he started to go with bad companions. He led a very sinful life with them. He learned many false doctrines at school also. His mother was very sad to see this change in her son. She prayed and prayed for him for twenty years.

God's plan for Augustine. All the time that Augustine was leading a sinful life, God was listening to his mother's prayers. God had His own way of bringing Augustine back to Him. All this time Augustine was not truly happy. He was looking for God, but was not looking in the right place.

Augustine left Africa in order to make a living in Rome.

Brown Brothers

Saint Augustine

He was not there very long when he became a teacher in Milan. There he heard the saintly Bishop Ambrose preaching. Saint Ambrose explained in his talks many things about the Christian religion that Saint Augustine had not understood before. He became a great lover of Saint Paul and took him as a special patron.

Saint Augustine was baptized by Saint Ambrose and became a very wonderful Christian. Like Saint Jerome and Saint Ambrose, his friends, he became very holy. It was not by chance that Augustine went to Milan as a teacher. God planned that he would meet Saint Ambrose there. God is always trying to bring us closer to Him.

Saint Monica was now very happy to see her son a Christian. She died shortly after this great event.

The scholar. Saint Augustine soon returned to Africa. There he wrote many books defending the Christian religion. The most famous of these is called the "City of God." It is really Augustine's masterpiece. It tells how happiness is found in love of God instead of in the love of self. It shows that the City of God is really heaven, not an earthly city. It tells how God's City will last forever and is perfect. Augustine had a brilliant mind and used it to spread the name of God.

The monk. When Augustine returned to Africa, he wanted to live ever more closely to God. So he turned his home into a monastery. There he and a few companions led a life of poverty and prayer. They lived very much the way monks live today.

In time Saint Augustine was ordained priest. Later he was made Bishop of Hippo in Africa. He and his priests lived a common life there just as he did before. The rule he wrote for them was the same for all. It emphasized most especially the virtue of charity.

Saint Augustine's sister became a religious also. While she was superior of her convent, he wrote a long letter telling her about the life and virtues of a true Sister. This letter has become very famous.

Many religious orders today follow a rule which is based on the Rule of Saint Augustine. Do you know the name of the rule followed by the Sisters in your school? You will read about some other religious rules in the next Unit.

Death of Saint Augustine. In 430, Saint Augustine died. The terrible Vandals, one of the Teuton tribes, were attacking Africa at this time. These Vandals destroyed much of the valuable Roman culture that was in Africa. We celebrate the feast of Saint Augustine on August 28.

Saint Augustine's ideas. This Saint had a great effect on the Church. He wrote many books which are still read today. He not only wrote books about the Holy Trinity and the Bible, but also on how to teach religion and how to live a good life.

Many times he wrote about how much God loves us, and how much we should love God in return.

Saint Augustine was also a great preacher. In his days a sermon might last two hours or more. The people did not sit down in church, as we do. They stood all the time. And yet Saint Augustine was so interesting a speaker that nobody seemed to get tired listening to him.

He often preached about the Bible and told the people the meaning of different parts of it. People still read Saint Augustine's sermons. Great scholars still study them. People know that Saint Augustine can teach them many things about the Bible and its meaning.

This great Saint also wrote many letters. He had a large number of friends. They often wrote to him and asked him to explain things about our holy religion. Then he would write a letter answering their questions. We can tell from Saint Augustine's letters that he must have loved his friends very much.

When you get older you will want to read some of Saint Augustine's writings. Although he wrote in Latin, most of his works have been translated into English.

Saint Augustine can teach all of us to love God more, and to be better Catholics.

Word Study

heresy	doctrine	Vulgate	scholars
virtue	monastery	Nicene Creed	

Testing Your Understanding

Number your paper 1 to 10. After each number write the correct answer for each of the following.

1. What do we call Christian writers of the first century?
2. Saint Ignatius was bishop of what important place?
3. Which of the Fathers is famous for his writings on the Holy Eucharist?
4. Who wrote the *City of God?*
5. What is the name of the Creed said at Holy Mass?
6. Where was Saint Augustine baptized?
7. Who defended the Church against Arianism in the West?
8. What is the name of the Bible in Latin?
9. Whom did the Bishop of Alex-

andria bring with him to the Council of Nicaea?

10. What do we call a false teaching about religion?

Review of Unit Four

Play a game with these. Read the first statement to your group. Give an extra point to each boy or girl in your group who can add something to what has been read on that topic. Appoint a boy or girl to keep the score. Then proceed to the next statement. Ten minutes before the period is over, the teacher will close the game. The winner of each group will be chairman for the game at the end of the next Unit, or sooner, if the teacher desires it.

1. The apostles helped Christ to spread the Gospel.
2. The Emperors said the Christians were enemies of the Empire.
3. The Christians suffered cruel treatment from the Emperors because they would not offer sacrifice to the false gods.
4. The Church grew stronger from the blood of the martyrs.
5. The Christians used the catacombs for refuge, burying their dead, and holding divine services.
6. Constantine gave full liberty to the Christians in 313.
7. Christianity became the religion of the Empire in 391. However, many pagans still believed in their false gods, although they had no pagan temples.
8. The great Roman Empire began to decay from within. Sin and evil was frequent; the government did not keep things in condition; there was no money coming into Rome.
9. People from the North became paid soldiers of Rome's army.
10. For the first four centuries, the barbarians were held back. They did not capture Rome.
11. In 410, Rome was sacked by Alaric, and precious treasures of art and culture stolen.
12. In 476, the Roman Empire in the West was captured. Rome fell and the barbarians became the rulers.
13. The Teutons began to rule Rome in 476. This is called the Fall of the Roman Empire.
14. The Empire was divided after the reign of Constantine. The Western Empire fell, but the Eastern Empire lasted a thousand years longer.
15. One of the greatest Eastern Emperors was Justinian. He collected all the laws and had them published. This work is called the Justinian Code or "Body of Civil Law."
16. The Church had early writers

who helped to correct wrong ideas about religion.

17. Saint Athanasius was a Doctor of the Church who lived in the East.
18. Saint Ambrose was a Doctor of the Church who was Bishop of Milan.
19. Saint Jerome wrote many wonderful works. His most famous work is the translation of the Bible into Latin.
20. The Latin translation of the Bible is called the Vulgate.
21. The Nicene Creed was composed at the Council of Nicaea in 325 A.D.
22. The greatest Doctor of the Church was Saint Augustine, Bishop of Hippo.

Have You Time to Do One or Two of These?

Your teacher will tell you whether you are to do one or more of these assignments.

1. Find out something about the Knights and Handmaids of the Blessed Sacrament. Why are these like Saint Tarcisius?
2. Write four sentences telling how Saint Maria Goretti is a martyr like Saint Agnes.
3. Plan a poster. Find pictures of martyrs of today in Europe. Paste them on the right-hand side of your poster. Paste pictures of the early martyrs on the left-hand side. Outline or paste a cross in the center of the pictures. Above write or letter these words: "Martyrs make the Church grow larger." In place of the cross you may substitute a picture of a large church or basilica, or a map with crosses to show the spread of the Church.
4. Prepare a "Who am I?" game. Write three sentences about some character in this Unit without mentioning the name. Then ask the class to guess the character you mentioned.
5. Pretend you are Saint Monica or Saint Augustine. Write a little story about what they must have talked about to each other.

Mastery Test of Unit Four

I. Fill in the blanks from the list of words given below:

God   Saint Peter   Saint Helena   Constantine   Jerome
deacons   Saint Leo   Ignatius of Antioch   Augustine   Ambrose

1. The apostles worked miracles by the power of _____.
2. _____ preached at Antioch, which became the first center of Christianity.
3. Men called _____ were

appointed to help the Apostles.

4. _____ showed her love for Christ by looking for the true Cross.

5. The Edict of Milan was published by _____.

6. Saint _____ wrote the *City of God*.

7. _____ protected the people from a barbarian attack on the city of Rome.

8. A Doctor of the Church who wrote the Vulgate is named Saint _____.

9. Saint _____ was martyred for Christ by being thrown to lions.

10. Saint Augustine was converted through the preaching of Saint _____

II. Copy the following terms in Column A on your paper. Write the phrase in Column B which best matches it.

Column A	Column B
1. Christianity	a. meeting of bishops of the Church
2. civilization	b. land governed by an emperor
3. catacombs	c. way of living, including customs, culture, education
4. Empire	d. the religion of Christians
5. Council	e. underground tunnels where Christians buried their dead

III. Divide your paper in two by drawing a line through the center from top to bottom. In Column I number the first ten lines. Write after each the correct answer to the following.

1. Who was the first deacon to be martyred?

2. Who was a disciple or pupil of Saint Polycarp?

3. Who made Christianity the religion of the Empire?

4. Who was called the "Scourge of God"?

5. What Gothic leader sacked Rome in 410 A.D.?

6. What sinner became a great saint and Doctor of the Church?

7. Who brought Holy Communion to the Christian prisoners?

8. What Roman soldier was pierced with arrows and martyred afterwards?

9. Who was the mother of Constantine?

10. Who was the mother of Augustine?

IV. In Column II of your paper write the word or words which complete each sentence below.

1. Justinian wrote the _____.
2. Saint _____ was crucified with his head down.
3. Saint John was the last of the Apostles to _____.
4. Saint _____ was burned to death on a gridiron.
5. There were about _____ hundred miles of catacombs underneath the city of Rome.
6. There is a _____ of a martyr in each altar stone upon which Mass is said to-day.
7. Saint _____ was known as the "Apostle of the Gentiles."
8. Pope Saint Leo saved Rome by visiting _____.
9. "Barrack Emperors" were those chosen by the _____.
10. Before Rome fell to the Teutons, it had _____ within itself.

V. Place these events in the order in which they happened.

Edict of Milan
Persecution of Christians
Barbarians sack Rome
The first martyr, Stephen
Barbarians belong to the Roman army
Pentecost

Do the same with these.

The end of the persecutions
Christianity becomes the religion of the Empire
Saint Agnes is martyred
The birth of Christ
The crucifixion of Christ

VI. Answer in complete sentences.

1. What do you mean by the Fall of the Roman Empire?
2. Why is Saint Augustine a great saint?
3. What did Saint Jerome do for the Church?
4. Name two Doctors of the Church who fought Arianism, one in the East and one in the West.
5. What is meant by Byzantine culture?
6. Who changed the name of the city of Byzantine?

Hymns to Mary

HISTORY OF HYMNS. Saint Alphonsus Liguori (1696–1762), the founder of the Redemptorist Order, was a theologian, a writer of devotional books, and a composer. He founded his Order to give missions to people in country districts, and he wrote hymns for them to sing. The hymns of Saint Alphonsus are contained in his many devotional works. About 1854 these hymns were collected into one volume, and English translations were made by the Redemptorist Father Edmund Vaughan. Saint Alphonsus was a fine musician, and some of his music is still heard, including some hymn tunes.

ORIGIN AND MEANING. The hymn "O Purest of Creatures," was written by Father Frederick William Faber. Father Faber wrote the hymn in 1854, when Mary was honored by a new title, that of the Immaculate Conception. The first and third stanzas of the hymn mention the Immaculate Conception. The rest of the hymn refers to the struggle between the Church and her enemies. This struggle was very bitter, especially in Europe. Many men hated the Church, and they hoped to destroy her if they could. This hymn appeals to Mary to protect the Church against these enemies.

O Purest of Creatures

O purest of creatures! Sweet Mother, sweet Maid!
The one spotless womb wherein Jesus was laid.
Dark night hath come down on us, Mother, and we
Look out for thy shining, sweet Star of the Sea.

Deep night hath come down on this rough-spoken world,
And the banners of darkness are boldly unfurled;
And the tempest-tossed Church, all her eyes are on thee,
They look to thy shining, sweet Star of the Sea.

He gazed on thy soul; it was spotless and fair;
For the empire of sin, it had never been there;
None had e'er owned thee, dear Mother, but He,
And He blessed thy clear shining, sweet Star of the Sea.

Earth gave Him one lodging; 'twas deep in thy breast,
And God found a home where the sinner finds rest.
His home and His hiding-place, both were in thee;
He was won by thy shining, sweet Star of the Sea.

APPLICATION. Mary, the Star of the Sea, is our guide through life by prayer and invocation. Mary, like a star, will guide us on the way to heaven, just as a voyage at sea has its danger if the ship is not held on its course by a navigator guided by the stars.

Courtesy of Rev. J. B. Carol, O. F. M.

UNIT FIVE

THE CHURCH SAVES CHRISTIAN CIVILIZATION

UNIT FIVE

THE CHURCH SAVES CHRISTIAN CIVILIZATION

You have been reading about the great challenge that came to Christian civilization. It came when tribes of barbarian peoples settled in the Roman Empire.

When this happened, the once great Roman Empire fell to pieces. It was no longer one great land governed by one ruler. In fact, the Empire changed so much that it no longer seemed like a civilized land.

The barbarians who ravaged or destroyed the Roman lands knew nothing about the Christian religion. They had always lived a wild and carefree life. No one had ever taught them how to live well. They knew little about taking care of their homes, their farms, their roads, or themselves.

So far, you have learned about the great thinkers of Greece and the great writers and lawmakers of Rome. All the culture of Greece and all the glorious arts of Rome were not appreciated by the barbarians. These things meant nothing to them.

It looked as if all the civilization of hundreds of years would be completely destroyed by the barbarians.

There was only one true society left which could save civilization for the world. That great institution, or society, was the Church.

What did the Church do to save Christian civilization? First, the Church raised up men who, by their holy living and careful study, would guard the civilization of the past.

CHAPTER I

IRISH MONKS AND MISSIONARIES

Looking into the chapter. You have been studying in Unit Four about the barbarians who overtook the Roman Empire. These barbarians were pagans. They knew very little or nothing about the civilization of the past years. They destroyed valuable works of art and precious writings.

This work of ruin went on throughout the Roman Empire. The barbarians did not know they were damaging things which they should cherish. They were never taught to love civilization. They had never heard about the one true God.

This was a difficult time for the world. All seemed lost. The work of centuries was almost wiped out.

But God did not allow this terrible thing to happen. God raised up in His Church a band of men who would preserve the finest things in the world during those barbarian invasions.

These men were called monks. They would begin to teach the barbarians the saving doctrines of Christianity.

This chapter tells about the first monks of the Church. It also tells how Irish monks preserved and spread civilization on the continent of Europe.

1. The First Christian Monks

About the third century, more and more men began to withdraw from the world. Some of them built small huts in the desert. There they lived a strict life of prayer and sacrifice. They did this for the love of God.

The first who lived this kind of life was named Saint Antony. He lived in the southern part of Egypt. Because he lived alone, he was called a monk, or hermit.

After a while, many people heard about the holiness of Saint Antony of Egypt. They,

Saint Antony in his cave in the desert

too, desired to live the same kind of life as he did. These people came to the desert also. Saint Antony taught them how to live as monks. They did not live together, but each monk had his own cell. In his own cell, each monk prayed, fasted, and did penance.

Another great monk of Egypt. A little later, there was another famous monk. He lived in northern Egypt. His name was Pachomius (pa-koe'-me-us). He made a rule for his monks. They lived in separate huts, just as the monks of Saint An-

tony did. But the monks met to say certain prayers each day. They also spent some time in manual labor. Because these monks led a common life, we say they lived a community life.

Not only monks practiced this kind of life. Women also came together to live as hermits. These women were called *nuns.*

Saint Basil's rule. Monastic life soon spread to Asia. There a Greek named Saint Basil began to live as a monk. He made a rule for his monks which was

Saint Basil

Culver Service

different from the Egyptian way of life. He built a house where all the monks lived together under one roof. He called this house a *monastery*. The rule of Saint Basil also called for a common life, where prayer and hard work had a place each day. Saint Basil is also one of the Fathers of the Church.

The rule of Saint Basil spread to Europe and especially to the kingdom of people called the Slavs. Even today, monks in the East follow the monastic life founded by Saint Basil.

Spread of the Egyptian rule for monks. In the Western part of

Europe, however, many people lived like Saint Pachomius and his monks. In the fifth century there were two famous monasteries of this type in Gaul. Today, this is called France. These monasteries were founded at Tours (toor) and Lerins (le-rin'). The monastery at Tours was founded by the bishop of that diocese. We all know him as Saint Martin of Tours. He loved the life of the monks, and he helped make the monastery grow.

2. Saint Patrick, Apostle of Ireland

In the monastery at Lerins there was a monk named Sucat. He was later called Patrick. He was born of Christian parents. Many people think that his mother was the niece of Saint Martin, Bishop of Tours.

Patrick, a slave. When Patrick was a young boy, he had been kidnapped. He was taken to Ireland. There, from the age of sixteen to twenty-two, he took care of sheep on the mountainsides.

While caring for the flock, Patrick studied the Irish language. He learned much about the pagan religion of the Irish people also. Patrick was a Christian. He loved these Irish people. He longed to tell these people about Christ.

Patrick, a monk. Finally, Patrick escaped from Ireland and reached France. There he entered the monastery at Lerins and studied to become a priest. When he received Holy Orders, he was given the name Patrick.

Patrick had one great ambition. He wanted to devote his life to converting the Irish. Soon after his ordination he visited Pope Celestine II. This Pope made Patrick a bishop in 432. He sent Patrick back to Ireland to make Christians out of the pagan Irish people.

So it was that Saint Patrick returned to Ireland, as a monk and a bishop. He was already familiar with the Irish language. So he started immediately to preach to the Irish chieftains about the true God.

Patrick, apostle. From the very beginning, Patrick was successful. He was given permission to preach everywhere in Ireland. Saint Patrick found Ireland a pagan country. At his death, he left it a Christian country. He brought with him men of every trade. These men worked for Saint Patrick. They built more than 300 churches in Ireland. He himself baptized about 160,000 people.

Culver Service

Saint Patrick in Ireland

It is said that an angel appeared to Saint Patrick just before his death. The angel promised him that Ireland would never lose the Christian Faith. Ireland has suffered very much for the Faith. But the people of Ireland have never given up or abandoned the Faith.

3. Work of the Monks in Ireland

The great work of Saint Patrick went on after his death in 461. When he ordained priests, they also became monks like Saint Patrick. These monks continued to follow the holy example and

An old Irish tower

But there was one bright spot in Europe. There was one hope for civilization. That was the Church, through the work of the monks. Ireland was completely converted before the Empire fell apart. No barbarians upset that land at that time.

These Irish monks kept and preserved the arts of civilization. They kept alive the civilization of the past. They knew Greek and Latin very well. They copied and recopied very carefully important writings. These copies, called *manuscripts,* were very beautifully colored and decorated.

From the sixth to the eighth century, the Irish monks were the chief scholars of all western Europe.

Not only did the monks study but they also taught. Every monastery had a monastic school attached to it. From all parts of Europe students came to these monastic schools. Here they were taught the great works of Greek and Latin writers. Here they learned the arts of Christian civilization that had been almost destroyed on the continent.

teachings of their great leader.

Land of saints. The strict and holy lives of these Irish monks were truly pleasing to God. They gave good example to those who learned about them. God prepared these monks to carry on the Christian religion when the Roman Empire was falling apart. God planned that the Irish monks would be ready to preach the Faith later in other lands.

Land of scholars. The world was terribly upset when Rome fell. Civilization was in danger. The barbarians did not care for civilization. These were the days that people sometimes call the "Dark Ages."

4. Irish Missionaries in Other Lands

Apostle of Scotland. Saint

Columba founded many churches in Ireland. He crossed over to Scotland, and began to convert the people there. He built a monastery on an island off the coast of Scotland. This island was named Iona. This monastery became one of the most famous monastic schools.

Before his death in 597 A.D., Saint Columba had converted the people of Scotland. He is called the "Apostle of Scotland."

Irish monks in England. In the northern part of England, there was a kingdom called Northumbria. The people were called Angles. They were one of the barbarian tribes. The king of this region had spent some time at Iona. He asked that some monks build monasteries in his land also.

An Irish monk named Saint Aidan was consecrated bishop and sent to England from Iona. He built a famous monastery at Lindisfarne, an island off the shore of England. Many other monasteries were established in Northumbria, by monks from Lindisfarne.

Monks on the continent of Europe. Saint Columba had among his followers a monk named Saint Columban (kol-um'-ban). He longed to convert the barbarian nations and teach them civilization.

He first preached among the people of Gaul, who were called Franks. He was very successful there for a while. Later, Saint Columban founded monasteries in France, Germany, Switzerland, and Italy. The last monastery was in Bobbio, Italy, where he died in 615.

A monastery in the Alps. High in the Alps in Switzerland, there is a monastery founded by Saint Gall, an Irish monk. A town grew around this monastic school and it also was called Saint Gall. The monks of this monastery made copies of valuable manuscripts. They preserved so many writings that it is said this monastery was one of the greatest places of learning in Europe. It has a very famous library. Saint Gall was a follower of Saint Columban.

5. Other Irish Saints

Many monasteries for nuns sprang up in Ireland at the time of Saint Patrick. Saint Brigid was the foundress of these nuns. Her famous monastery was at Kildare.

Another famous Irish monk was Saint Brendan. He founded many monasteries also. It is said that he made many journeys by sea. People called him "Brendan, the Voyager." He made many journeys to other lands, exploring as he went along. Saint Brendan was really ahead of his time. No one thought of exploring new lands in those days. Later on, people like the Northmen explored and made famous discoveries. We have accounts of Saint Brendan's long voyages. However, we are not certain as to what lands were really discovered by Saint Brendan, the Voyager.

Can you understand why this Unit is important? It shows what a debt civilization owes to the Catholic Church. It points out that, without the work of the monks, civilization would have died out. There would have been no one to teach the barbarians in other lands about Christianity.

Words to Study

manuscript   monk   monastery   hermit   voyager

What Is The Word?

Try to supply the correct word for each statement.

1. A nation which began to receive Christianity in 432 was _____.

2. Saint Patrick had converted his people completely even before the fall of _____.

3. While Europe was overrun by barbarians, _____ kept Christian civilization alive.

4. The first Christian monks lived in _____ in Africa.

5. The first hermit was _____ of _____.

6. Two famous monasteries in Gaul were _____ and _____.

7. Saint Patrick was a monk and bishop who brought _____ to Ireland.

8. Saint Columba is the Apostle of _____, whose famous monastery was _____.

9. Saint Aidan was an Irish monk who established a monastery at _____.

10. Saint _____ spread Irish monastic life in Europe, France, Germany, Switzerland, and Italy.

11. The monastery of Saint Gall, in _____, is famous for its library and learning.

CHAPTER II

MONKS OF SAINT BENEDICT

Keeping the threads together. In this Unit you are learning how civilization survived the invasions. It survived because of the work of the monks of the Church. You have read of the work of the Irish monks. Other monks also were great teachers. These monks were followers of Saint Benedict.

These monks spent much time teaching the barbarians how to live like civilized people. They showed them how to take care of their farms and grow certain crops. The monks themselves spent a certain amount of time each day working.

In this chapter, you will read more about the great Saint Benedict, and the work of many of his famous monks.

1. Founder of Monks in the West

Saint Benedict was born in Italy, in a place called Nursia (nur'-see-a), in the sixth century. In his boyhood days, he was sent to Rome to be educated. At the age of fourteen, he left the world and went to live alone in a cave. There he spent his time praying and fasting. He was living at a place called Subiaco (soo-bee-ah'-co). Many others came to join him in leading a holy life.

Later, in 520, he moved his band of followers to a hill called Monte Cassino (mon'-tay cah-see'-no). There Saint Benedict wrote his famous rule for monks, called the Benedictine Rule. He named his monastery after Saint Martin of Tours.

The Rule of the Benedictines was very simple. It called for a life of prayer and work. Besides living a holy life himself, the monk must give an example of goodness and holiness to others.

The monks recited the Divine Office each day. The Divine Office is a collection of prayers

175

Saint Benedict

Saint Benedict said that everyone was to be treated as if he were Christ Himself. No one was to be turned away from a Benedictine monastery.

The monks did this work for the love of God. Those who work for the love of God practice true charity. That is what Saint Benedict commanded his monks to do.

Kinds of work done by the Benedictines. The Benedictine monks spent a certain amount of time each day at work. Many of them worked in the fields around the monastery. They grew crops and cultivated them. Some of the monks were artists and sculptors. Others worked at different kinds of trades.

The barbarians learn how to live. People began to build homes around the monasteries. The barbarians came to the monks for help. The monks taught the people how to farm. They taught the people how to build good roads, canals, buildings, and bridges. In this way the monks taught the barbarians that it is better to work than to be idle or to be fighting in useless wars.

The monasteries needed books for Mass, called missals. They also needed other books

and psalms which praise and glorify God. The monks called the chanting of the Office a "work of God."

Monasteries, homes and charity. In the Middle Ages, there were no hospitals. People were cared for at the monastery by the monks. Whenever people were in any kind of trouble, they came to the monastery for help. The poor, the hungry, and the needy found help in the monasteries.

There were no hotels or inns in Europe in those days. Travelers would stop at monasteries for rest and shelter. Everyone who came was received kindly.

Scene inside a monastery today

from which they could recite the Divine Office. The monks spent time preparing these books. They also trained their monks to become priests. After some time, there was a part of each day set apart for study by the rule. Soon schools became attached to the Benedictine monasteries, just as each Irish monastery had a school.

The monks were the most educated people of the Middle Ages. Their monasteries were the centers of civilization at that time. Benedictine monasteries spread throughout every section of Europe.

Life of the Benedictine monks. The rule of Saint Benedict stated that the monks take vows. These vows were serious promises to God. The monks promised to own no personal property, not to marry, and to obey the superior of the monastery. The monks led a life in common. The superior was called an *abbot,* which means "father." The abbot had the great responsibility of seeing to it that the monks carried out the motto, "to labor is to pray."

Before printing was invented, books had to be copied by hand

2. Pope Saint Gregory the Great

In Rome at this time there lived a Roman patrician. He came from a rich and noble family and had been raised to the highest public office in Rome. Soon after this, he gave up his fine position, gave his wealth to the poor, and became a monk of Saint Benedict. This monk was named Gregory.

Gregory founded six monasteries and made his own former home into a monastery. There he lived as abbot for a time. Then the Pope sent for him and gave him several important offices of trust.

Finally, the Pope died in 590 and Gregory was elected the next Pope. He was the first monk to become Pope. Gregory did so much for the Church during the years of his reign he has been called Gregory the Great.

Doctor of the Church. Pope Gregory wrote so many valuable works on religion that he was made a Doctor of the Church. He wrote books which explained difficult things in simple language that everyone could understand.

Love of law and order. Gregory the Great had love for law and

Culver Service
Pope Gregory the Great

order. We say that as Pope, he was a good organizer. While he was Pope, the Lombards began to invade Italy. There was no emperor in Rome to raise an army to keep them out. So Gregory himself raised an army and fought the Lombards. Finally, he made them sign a truce. In this treaty the Lombards were to settle down and make war no longer. After this the Lombards caused no more trouble.

Pope Gregory did even more for the Church. The Goths who lived in the West were called *Visigoths*. They had finally settled in Spain. Because of Saint Gregory, their king became a Christian. Soon all the members of the Visigoths became Christians also. In this way, Gregory helped to spread Christianity and civilization.

The music that was used in the church services was called "plain chant." Saint Gregory collected all the chants that were being used in the Church and put them in order. Because of this, the plain chant is often called "Gregorian Chant."

Conversion of barbarians. Besides his work for the Lombards and Visigoths, Pope Saint Gregory helped the barbarians to become Christians.

Angles for sale. One day, before Gregory became Pope, he was walking through the streets of Rome. There he saw a number of boys being sold as slaves. They were handsome-looking boys, with light hair, fair skin and blue eyes. He asked who they were. The answer was that they were Angles. The Angles lived in the country we call England today. Gregory thought for a minute. Then he said, "No, not Angles, but angels. Soon the praise of God will be sung in their land so that their fair souls may become angels in heaven." Gregory meant that he wanted to go to their land to convert

179

Saint Augustine of Canterbury preaching about the Catholic faith

the people there to Christianity.

Gregory longed to preach the word of God in England. However, the Pope needed him in Rome for important things. But when Gregory became Pope, he remembered his friends among the Angles. He really did something to show his love for them.

Saint Gregory sent forty monks from his own Benedictine monastery in Rome to England. At the head of this band of monks, there was a learned and holy bishop named Augustine.

This group set sail for England in 597 A.D., happy to carry Christ's message to a strange land.

3. Saint Augustine of Canterbury

England had received word of the Gospel long before Saint Augustine came there. The Romans brought Christianity there in the beginning. But the Romans left to fight barbarians on the continent about 407. When they left, Christianity died out there. Some tribes of barbarians took over England in 449. These tribes were the Angles and the Saxons. These people were pagan and had never heard about the Christian religion. These were the people to whom Saint Augustine was sent in 597.

When Saint Augustine arrived, these tribes had set up seven kingdoms in England. He preached first in the kingdom of Kent, to a king named Ethelbert. He found that Latin was no longer the common language there, as it was in Roman lands. Now the people spoke a language that was a mixture of Latin and the language of the Angles and Saxons. This language is called Anglo-Saxon.

Conversion of the king. Bertha was the wife of Ethelbert. She was a Christian princess from a Frankish kingdom in Europe. Saint Augustine preached at Canterbury, which was the capital city of Kent. The king was converted and also the people of his kingdom. Thus it was that Saint Augustine was called Augustine of Canterbury. Canterbury became the center of Christianity in England.

Soon afterwards, Augustine began to preach to the people of the other kingdoms in England. More missionaries were needed. Saint Gregory sent forty more Benedictine monks to England to help in this great work.

Benedictine monasteries in England. While the Anglo-Saxons were being converted, there sprang up several monasteries of Benedictines in England. At Whitby there was a monastery of nuns and one of priests.

In 664, a meeting was held of Irish and Benedictine monks. At this meeting, it was decided that all the monasteries and churches in England would celebrate great feast-days on the same day that these were being celebrated in Rome. In other things also, England would follow the customs in Rome. Because this meeting was held at Whitby, it is known as the Council of Whitby.

4. Saint Boniface, the Saxon

In the beginning of the eighth century there was a monk in England named Winfrid. Winfrid was a Saxon who had joined the Benedictines. He worked for a while with Saint Willibrord in a part of Germany. Then he moved farther on. He made many converts among the barbarians in northwestern Germany. The Pope changed his name to Boniface, which means "doer

Saint Boniface cuts down the oak tree. Can you tell why he did this?

of good." Boniface built a famous monastery at Fulda, Germany.

While Boniface was working among the Germans, he did a very brave act. This act, however, won for him many more converts to the Faith.

The Germans had an oak tree which they regarded as very sacred. They believed that their god, named Thor, would kill anyone who did not honor this sacred tree. Boniface had no fear of a pagan god. Boniface chopped down the sacred tree while the German people looked on. Of course, nothing happened to Boniface. The people knew then that their god Thor did not exist. It showed the people that the religion of Boniface must be the true religion. Boniface used the wood of the oak tree to build a chapel.

Boniface, the Archbishop. Later, Boniface saw Germany divided into dioceses. He himself was appointed archbishop of Mainz (main'-tse). He did so much good for the Church in Germany that he is called the "Apostle of Germany."

Death of Boniface. One day,

while Boniface was preparing to give Confirmation to a group of people, a band of pagans entered and murdered him. He died in the year 754.

5. Bede, the Scholar

One of the most famous of all the early Benedictines was the Venerable Bede. He was educated at the monastery of Wearmouth-Jarrow in England. While still young, he entered the Benedictine Order and was ordained a priest.

Bede is famous, however, for a work that was quite different from that of Boniface and Augustine. Bede was really the first great English scholar.

The Venerable Bede had a thorough knowledge of Greek and Latin. He had both good training and fine intelligence. He wrote several books, all of which were useful. He wrote books explaining passages in the Bible, or Scripture. His books were used later as textbooks in schools.

Bede's history book. The most famous book that Bede gave us is his history book. It did not contain all the information of your history book. It contained the history of the English people up to the time of Bede. It was the best history written in Europe until the twelfth or thirteenth century.

Do You Know the Meaning of These Words?

Scripture   missals   Visigoths   scholar

Matching Test

Match correctly the names in Column A with the phrases in Column B.

Column A	*Column B*
Saint Augustine of Canterbury	the first great English scholar
Saint Boniface	apostle of Germany
Saint Benedict	brought Christianity to Spain
Pope Gregory the Great	brought Christianity to England
Venerable Bede	founder of monks in the West

For Discussion

1. How did Saint Gregory take part in the conversion of England?
2. Why did the Benedictine monks establish so many monasteries in Europe after Saint Gregory became Pope?
3. Why is Venerable Bede famous?

The Most Important Facts

Below are the most important facts contained in this Unit. You must be able to give three or four important sentences about each one of them to show you understand each fact very well.

1. The first monk to live by himself was Saint Antony of Egypt.
2. Followers of Saint Pachomius led a common life in Upper Egypt.
3. Saint Basil's monks began to live in one large building, called a monastery.
4. Saint Basil's rule is still followed by the monks in the East.
5. There were two monasteries in Gaul which followed the Rule of Saint Pachomius.
6. Saint Patrick lived in Gaul, at the monastery called Lerins.
7. Saint Patrick obtained permission from Pope Celestine to convert the Irish.
8. Saint Patrick successfully converted Ireland and established monastic life there.
9. The Irish monks led holy lives and taught the ways of civilization in their schools.
10. The Irish monks kept alive the learning of the past by copying and studying Greek and Latin manuscripts.
11. Saint Columba is called the Apostle of Scotland.
12. Saint Columban founded many monasteries in France, Germany, Switzerland, and Italy.
13. Saint Gall founded a monastery in Switzerland, which is famous for its learning.
14. Saint Aidan founded a monastery in England at Lindisfarne.
15. Saint Brendan founded many monasteries and explored many other lands at an early period of history.
16. Saint Benedict founded an order of monks at Monte Cassino, Italy.
17. The Benedictine monks taught the barbarians how to farm, build roads, and become civilized in every way.
18. Saint Gregory was the first monk to become a Pope.
19. Saint Gregory was a Doctor

of the Church and one who knew how to make laws and keep order.

20. Saint Gregory sent Saint Augustine of Canterbury to convert the Angles in England.

21. Saint Boniface is called the Apostle of Germany.

22. The first great English scholar was the Benedictine monk named Venerable Bede.

Things to Do

Prepare a radio talk of one paragraph on "Saints Who Spread the Gospel." Base your talk on the saints you learned about during this Unit.

On an outline map of Europe write or letter the names of these important places: Lerins, Iona, Kent, Monte Cassino, St. Gall, Wearmouth-Jarrow.

Compare Saint Augustine, the Doctor of the Church, whom you studied in Unit Four, and Saint Augustine, the Archbishop of Canterbury in England. Use the following questions as your guide.

1. Were they born in the same country?
2. Did they live in the same century?
3. Were they both monks? If so, were they monks in the same country?
4. Were Saint Ambrose and Saint Gregory friendly to both of them?
5. Did they both write books about religion?
6. Did they both convert the English?

Fill in the following chart on another paper: (Some are already filled in for your benefit).

Name of Saint	Title	Office in the Church	Famous Work or Famous Monastery
1. Patrick	Apostle of Ireland		
2. Columba			
3. Antony		Hermit	Lived a holy life in the desert
4. Basil		Monk	Wrote a rule for monks in East
5. Columban		Monk	(Name countries where he labored)
6. Boniface			
7. Gall			
8. Benedict			
9. Gregory			
10. Augustine			

Mastery Test for Unit Five

I. Who was he?

Select the name of the person described in each sentence. Write each answer on your paper in complete sentences. You may use some names for answers more than once.

Saint Augustine	Saint Boniface
Saint Patrick	Saint Gall
Saint Columba	Venerable Bede
Saint Gregory	Saint Benedict
Saint Antony	Saint Basil
Saint Aidan	Saint Pachomius

1. He converted the Visigoths in Spain.
2. He made an oak tree into a chapel.
3. The center of his work was at Canterbury in England.
4. He founded a monastery at Monte Cassino.
5. He taught that to labor was to pray.
6. He wrote an early history of England.
7. He founded a monastery at Iona.
8. He wrote a rule followed to-day by monks in the East.
9. He founded a monastery at Lindisfarne.
10. He was the first monk to become Pope.
11. He was the first monk to lead a life of prayer and fasting in the desert.
12. He founded a monastery in Switzerland.
13. He started common life for monks in Upper Egypt.
14. He began monastic life in Ireland.
15. He put all the chants in order and assembled them in a book.
16. He received a fine schooling at Wearmouth-Jarrow.
17. His name was Winfrid before the Pope changed it.
18. He first converted the people of Kent in England.
19. He founded monastic life in the West.
20. He was a Saxon who became a Benedictine.

II. Arrange these events in the order in which they took place. Place 1, 2, 3, 4, 5 after each one on your paper after you have copied the entire exercise.

...... Saint Patrick brought Christianity to Ireland.

...... Saint Boniface went to Germany.

...... Saint Benedict wrote his rule at Monte Cassino.

...... The Council of Whitby was held in England.

...... Saint Columban died at Bobbio, Italy.

III. Answer the following questions.

1. Where was Saint Boniface's famous monastery in Germany?

2. Who wanted to go himself to convert the Angles?

3. What land was called the "Isle of Saints and Scholars?"

4. What name did the Pope give to Winfrid?

5. What saint went back to convert the people who made him a slave?

6. What were copies of famous writings called?

7. Who built many monasteries in Scotland?

8. To what people did Saint Columban first preach?

9. What saint founded monasteries for nuns in Ireland?

10. Where did Saint Benedict write his famous Rule?

11. What does the word "abbot" mean?

12. Who raised an army and made peace with the Lombards?

13. In what country did the Angles live?

14. What place in England was the center of the Christian religion?

15. Did the monks own personal property?

16. Was Bede a Benedictine or an Irish monk?

17. Was Boniface or Augustine a Saxon?

18. What was the motto of the Benedictine monks?

19. At what monastery did Saint Patrick live in France?

20. What Pope did much to organize Church music?

21. In what year did Saint Patrick begin the conversion of Ireland?

22. What barbarian nation besides the Saxons was invading England about 449?

23. To which kingdom did Saint Augustine go to preach Christianity?

24. What are the ages after the barbarian invasions sometimes called?

25. Who gave the greatest service to the world by guarding Christian civilization?

Hymns to Mary

HISTORY OF HYMNS. Father Frederick William Faber (1814–1863) is probably the outstanding author of English hymns. He knew that hymns can help people take part in church services. Father Faber saw the need for English hymns, and so he composed many of them. It was in London that he wrote many of his hymns. Among these are, "Jesus, My Lord, My God, My All," "Dear Guardian of Mary," and, "Hail, Glorious Saint Patrick."

ORIGIN AND MEANING. The hymn, "Hail, Queen of Heaven, the Ocean Star," was composed by a very famous Catholic leader and historian. His name was Father John Lingard. This hymn was written about 1840 and is in a book called "A Manual of Prayers." This hymn is similar in some ways to the "Salve Regina." All of you know the "Salve Regina" as the "Hail, Holy Queen" which is recited after Low Mass. In both hymns we are called wanderers in a vale of tears. It is to Mary, our gracious and blest Advocate, that we turn for comfort. The last line of each stanza tells for whom we pray when we sing this hymn.

Hail, Queen of Heaven, the Ocean Star

Hail, Queen of heaven, the ocean Star,
  Guide of the wanderer here below!
Thrown on life's surge we claim thy care,
  Save us from peril and from woe.
Mother of Christ, Star of the Sea,
  Pray for the wanderer, pray for me!

O gentle, chaste and spotless Maid,
  We sinners make our prayers through thee!
Remind thy Son that He has paid
  The price of our iniquity.
Virgin most pure, Star of the Sea,
  Pray for the sinner, O pray for me!

Sojourners in this vale of tears
  To thee, blest Advocate, we cry,
Pity our sorrows, calm our fears,
  And soothe with hope our misery,
Refuge in grief, Star of the Sea,
  Pray for the mourner, O pray for me.

And while to Him who reigns above,
  In Godhead One, in persons three,
The source of life, of grace, of love,
  Homage we pay on bended knee—
Do thou bright Queen, Star of the Sea,
  Pray for thy children, pray for me!

APPLICATION. Mary, Mother Most amiable, humbly accepted the honor of being the Mother of Jesus.

We must be willing to live the life that God desires, accepting the pleasures and pains according to the example set by Mary.

Courtesy of Rev. J. B. Carol, O. F. M.

UNIT SIX

FEUDALISM MOLDS CHRISTIAN CIVILIZATION

CHAPTER I—THE FRANKS BUILD AN EMPIRE

Conversion of Clovis
Victory of Charles Martel
Founding of the Papal States
Charlemagne Revives Civilization
Coronation of Charlemagne

CHAPTER II—CASTLES, KNIGHTS, AND NOBLES

Meaning of Feudalism
Ceremony of Homage
Castles in the Middle Ages
Steps to Knighthood

CHAPTER III—FEUDALISM ON THE CONTINENT

The Empire Is Divided
The Church Tries to Keep Peace
Three Famous Kings
Early Rulers of Germany
Emperor of Germany and Italy

CHAPTER IV—BEFORE THE NORMANS CAME TO ENGLAND

Land of Invasions
When England Was Angle-land
Rule of Alfred the Great
The Norman Victory

CHAPTER V—LIBERTY UNDER THE MAGNA CARTA

Rule of William the Conqueror
Henry II Restores Order
Henry II and Common Law
John, a Cruel King and Tyrant
The Signing of the Magna Carta

UNIT SIX

FEUDALISM MOLDS CHRISTIAN CIVILIZATION

You have seen what a change took place in Rome after the barbarian tribes overran it. But the Church did not fail when Rome was taken. The Church will last till the end of time because it has a Divine Founder, Jesus Christ.

The Church is the mother of all peoples on earth. The Church began the work of making Christians out of these pagan peoples. Not only did the Church make them heirs of heaven but she also civilized them.

Soon some of the tribes became strong enough to rule the new lands where they had settled. The Franks had a large empire. England was ruled for a while by Saxon kings, Danish kings, and Norman kings. Other kings ruled Germany.

After the death of Charlemagne, there was no king in France or Germany strong enough to raise an army and protect his people. The rich nobles took more and more power for themselves. They raised their own armies. Soon they had taken over large sections of land. They ruled these lands and the people who lived there. This rule by powerful nobles is called feudalism (few'-dal-ism).

Feudalism lasted in France and Germany for many years. No king did very much to break the power of the nobles and make himself the powerful leader of his people. Later on, kings became powerful, and we shall see how the people protected themselves against unjust demands of certain rulers.

CHAPTER I

THE FRANKS BUILD AN EMPIRE

Points to remember. In the previous Unit you learned that the Church saved civilization from being lost. You saw that various tribes of Teutons were making their homes in the Roman Empire. The Lombards finally made their homes in the northern part of Italy. The East Goths lived in the southern part.

What was happening to the rest of the old Roman Empire? Was there any ruler to take the place of the Roman Emperor? Would any of the Teutonic tribes become a part of Christian civilization?

This chapter tells the story of the barbarian tribe which became the most powerful. It tells about a tribe known as the Franks. This tribe became the first to practice the Christian religion. This chapter shows how the Franks defeated many other tribes and became the rulers of a large empire.

1. Conversion of Clovis

The Franks lived first in the lands now known as France, Belgium, and Holland. These tribes were not united. Each tribe was ruled by its own king.

About the year 485, some of the Franks crossed the Rhine River and settled in Gaul. This was part of the old Western Empire. The Franks were very good fighters. They often went to battle with only a sword or battle-ax for a weapon.

One king for all Franks. About 481 A.D. Clovis (kloe'-vis) became king of one of the Frankish tribes. He was very young, but he was a real leader. He was able to unite all the Frankish tribes under his rule. So, instead of many kings over small groups of Franks, there was one king of the Franks.

Clovis was just toward the tribes he united under his rule. He respected their laws and customs. He permitted them to keep their property. In this way Clovis gained their friendship. He worked for the good of everyone.

Clovis prays for victory. The wife of Clovis was a Christian. Her name was Clotilda. She often spoke to her husband about his becoming a Christian. But Clovis kept on worshipping the gods of the Franks.

One day Clovis was at war with some neighboring Teutons. Things were going badly for Clovis and his army. Clovis prayed to his pagan god for victory. The battle only became worse. He feared he would lose all his soldiers.

At this point he decided to call upon the true God. He asked God to help him. Clovis promised he would become a Christian if he obtained victory. Clovis gained a great victory. He remained true to his promise and became a Christian. Not only Clovis but all his army and the people of his kingdom became Christians.

Clovis was baptized by Saint Remigius (re-me'-jee-us), the Bishop of Rheims (rems). This bishop had instructed Clovis in the Christian religion. Clovis' baptism took place on Christmas Day, 496 A.D.

King Clovis was the first and

Brown Brothers
Baptism of Clovis

only Christian king in Western Europe at that time. His kingdom was the first to become entirely Christian. Before his death, the Frankish kingdom extended east beyond the Rhine River and almost as far south as Spain. France, so early converted, is often called eldest daughter of the Church.

2. Victory of Charles Martel

After the death of Clovis, his kingdom was divided among his four sons. These men were not good rulers. They were too weak to control their lands.

They did very little ruling but allowed their officers to manage affairs for them. The chief of these officers was called Mayor of the Palace. In time of war, the Mayor of the Palace usually led the army into battle.

A new enemy. About the beginning of the eighth century, a new enemy of Christianity appeared in Europe. This enemy was a new religion started by a man named Mohammed.

Life of Mohammed. Mohammed was born in Arabia, in the city of Mecca. He had been a camel driver in a caravan. While on his journeys, he picked up ideas about the Jewish and Christian religions from the travelers. He mixed these ideas up with some pagan ideas to form his own religion.

Mohammed was a fiery leader and a clever teacher. His followers were called Mohammedans. These people believed that Allah was their God and Mohammed was his prophet. Sometimes this religion is called Islam, which means "obedience to God's will."

The Mohammedan religion spreads. The Mohammedans claimed it was necessary to spread their new religion by force. They conquered all of Arabia and took possession of Jerusalem and the Holy Land. Next they conquered all of Northern Africa.

The Mohammedans of Africa were known as Moors. In 711, they entered Europe for the first time. They sent an army into Spain. Not only the Visigoths but the entire peninsula was conquered by them. They settled down in Spain for a while. Among the many fine buildings which they built in Spain was the *Alhambra,* in the city of Granada.

After a short time, the Moors began moving again. They started north from Spain. It looked as if Christian Europe would be overcome by this new enemy.

One brave leader appeared, named Charles Martel. As a

In a Moorish castle

Screen Traveler, from Gendreau

194

soldier, he struck at the enemy so hard, people called him "the Hammer." That is what Martel means. He was Mayor of the Palace in the Frankish kingdom at that time. He was loved and respected by the people. Although he was not the king, he did the king's work in ruling the Franks.

Christian civilization is saved. Charles Martel gathered a large army and prepared to fight this new enemy. The Franks and the Moors met at Tours. Can you find this place on your map?

A fierce battle took place. Charles completely defeated the Moors and drove them back to Spain.

This battle of Tours took place in 732 A.D. It was one of the most important battles in history. It was here that a Christian leader saved the world from Mohammedan rule. Christian civilization itself was saved from Mohammedanism.

3. Founding of the Papal States

Shortly after the Battle of Tours, Charles Martel died. His son, Pepin the Short, became

Charles Martel at the Battle of Tours

Mayor of the Palace. Pepin knew he would be the real ruler of the kingdom. He thought he should be called king. He called an assembly of nobles to elect him king. The Pope approved this act.

Pepin then set aside the last of the kings, called "do-nothing" kings. He was crowned King Pepin I by Saint Boniface. He was anointed king just as Saul and David had been anointed in olden times. The friendship between the Church and government grew stronger at this time.

The Franks defeat the Lombards. During Pepin's reign, trouble began with the Lombards. They tried to capture Rome. They had no right whatever to this land. The Holy Father at that time was Pope Stephen II. He tried to check the Lombards but was not successful. Then he called upon the Franks to help him.

King Pepin finally defeated the Lombards. In return he claimed a part of the land he had conquered.

King Pepin's gift. King Pepin did not want the land for himself. He said, "I have fought because I love the Church of Rome and to obtain pardon for my sins. I will give these lands to Saint Peter and his successors."

These lands which Pepin gave to the Pope are called the Papal States. They helped to supply money for charity and missionary work. This gift made the Pope a civil ruler. The Pope does not have to be a civil ruler. His real work is to be the spiritual leader of the whole world. However, it is helpful that our Holy Father should be independent of other rulers. By being independent of other rulers, he can use better his power as spiritual leader.

4. Charlemagne Revives Civilization

Pepin died about 768. The next great ruler was his son, Charles. He became one of the greatest rulers the world has ever known. The French called him Charlemagne (shar'-le-main), which means Charles the Great.

Charlemagne tried to rule in a Christian way. He united the tribes he conquered. He set a wonderful example for his people to follow.

Charlemagne conquered other tribes. The Lombards again started raiding Italy. Charlemagne set out immediately for northern Italy. There he de-

196

feated the Lombards. He then had himself crowned King of the Lombards. All the land of the Lombard people became part of the Frankish kingdom.

This was only the beginning of Charlemagne's wars. He turned his army towards the north, against the Saxons. These Saxons were a fierce tribe of Teutons. Charlemagne had a difficult time in Saxony, but he came out the winner in the end. Saxony is part of the land called Germany today. All this land became part of the Frankish kingdom.

South of Saxony there was a land called Bavaria. This land also was conquered by Charlemagne.

In the valley of the Danube River, towards the west, there lived a tribe that did not belong to the Teuton family. These people were called Avars. Their lands soon fell into the hands of Charlemagne.

Protection for the kingdom. Charlemagne set about protecting his kingdom. He set up a system of government for all the lands on the borders of his kingdom. These bordering territories were called "Marches." The military district called the Eastern March later became the country of Austria.

One enemy unconquered. Charlemagne was a very determined leader. He made up his mind to conquer the Moors in Spain. His soldiers, however, suffered a great defeat in Spain. Charlemagne's army has been made famous by a poem written about the war in Spain. The name of the poem is "The Song of Roland."

Charlemagne was not completely without a victory in Spain. He took the city of Barcelona and the land north of it. This he established as the "Spanish March." Do you think Charlemagne needed this protection on the south of his kingdom? Why?

Charlemagne

The Coronation of Charlemagne

5. Coronation of Charlemagne

By the year 800, Charlemagne had gained control of most of the land that had been the old Western Empire. But he did not live in Rome. He had a beautiful palace in the north of his kingdom at Aachen (Ah'-ken). Some people called it Aix-la-Chapelle (eks-la-sha-pel').

Charlemagne had done much for the Church. He protected the Christian religion and sent missionaries into the lands he conquered. In this way Christianity spread throughout his lands.

An important ceremony. On Christmas Day, 800, Charlemagne was crowned Emperor by Pope Leo III. This coronation took place in St. Peter's Church in Rome. The Roman people were very happy about this. The Western Empire now had an Emperor again. The people looked upon Charlemagne as the true successor of the old Roman Emperors. But they knew that Charlemagne's Empire was not exactly like the old Roman Empire. The old Roman Empire was pagan. This new Empire was a Christian Empire. That is why it came to be called the Holy Roman Empire.

Charlemagne promised to protect the Church and the Pope. He promised to do all he could to help spread a knowledge of our holy faith.

Laws of Charlemagne. Charlemagne had a great respect for laws. He believed in just laws. This was good for the world. It helped to prepare the way for democracy in America later on.

Charlemagne allowed every tribe to keep its own laws, if these were just and reasonable. He did not tax the people in order to support himself or his own palace. The people admired Charlemagne for these things.

Charlemagne did, however, make some laws which had to be kept by all. These laws were famous. They were called *capitularies*. Among the most famous of these laws were those on the education of the people.

Charlemagne called a meeting once every year. This meeting was called a *Mayfield*. At this meeting he allowed his people to discuss the laws which he had written down. The people could make suggestions about these laws.

Charlemagne divided his empire into districts. Over each district he placed a ruler called a *count*. Charlemagne wanted to be sure that every count was doing his duty. He sent out two men each year to each district. These men were called *missi*. They had to inspect the district to find out if the laws were being kept. Then they reported to Charlemagne.

Education in the time of Charlemagne. When Charlemagne was a boy, he did not go to school. There were few schools in Europe at that time, and these were usually monastic schools. Charlemagne was a grown man before he learned to read. He practiced writing at night, when he could not sleep. Yet he never learned to write any more than a few words.

Charlemagne, however, believed in education and understood its value. He was so fond of learning that during his meals he had someone read to him.

Charlemagne opened a school in his palace at Aachen. The children of the nobles and his own children attended this famous school. Sometimes Charlemagne himself attended classes and asked the teachers many questions.

The very best of teachers in Europe were appointed to teach in the palace school of Charlemagne. These teachers were English, Irish, Italians, and Spaniards. Some of them were Franks who had been educated at famous monasteries. The greatest of Charlemagne's teachers was Alcuin (al'-quin), a Benedictine monk from England.

All over his empire Charlemagne ordered schools to be established. Many of these schools had teachers who were trained by the Irish or Anglo-Saxon monks.

Charlemagne's cathedral. Charlemagne built a church at Aachen, where he lived. He brought the material for this building from Rome and Ravenna, because there were no precious metals among the Franks or tribes he conquered. The church was built in Eastern style, called Byzantine.

Charlemagne's plans. Charlemagne hoped to establish peace in his empire. He tried to protect the Pope. Charlemagne believed that good government meant that the Emperor and the Pope would work together for the good of men. The Emperor would govern the state. The Pope would govern spiritual affairs of the people.

Charlemagne worked closely with the Pope. He also was supposed to do all he could to help spread Christianity and protect the Church. That is why he was called the Holy Roman Emperor. That is why the empire was called the Holy Roman Empire.

The emperors who came after Charlemagne did not follow out Charlemagne's ideas. First of all, they did not have as much power as he had. They were emperors in name only. Then, too, some of them quarrelled with the Pope and refused to obey him.

As we have seen, Charlemagne did a great deal to help Christian education. He did a great deal to help the Church and the Pope. We must remember that Charlemagne was a pioneer in helping civilize much of Europe.

For these reasons he was truly a great man. He had certain faults, but in general he tried to do the best he could.

People still honor the memory of Charlemagne. There are many statues of him in Europe. Some people think that if Charlemagne's ideas would have been followed, there would not be so many wars today.

For Discussion

1. Why is Charles Martel remembered as a great man?

2. How did Charlemagne show his interest in learning?

Word Study

revives	Islamism	*missi*	manuscripts
Mohammedanism	Mayfield	capitularies	Papal States

Matching Test. Write sentences on your paper by matching Column A with Column B.

Column A	*Column B*
1. Clotilda	a. was crowned Holy Roman Emperor in 800
2. Charles Martel	b. gave the Papal States to the Pope
3. Mohammed	c. led the Franks to Christianity
4. Pepin	d. baptized King Clovis
5. Charlemagne	e. defeated the Mohammedans at Tours
6. Saint Remigius	f. was Christian wife of Clovis
7. Clovis	g. started a religion of his own

A Yes-No Test

Answer on your paper in complete sentences.

1. Did Clovis become a convert?

2. Was Mohammedanism a Christian religion?

3. Was Alcuin a famous teacher at Charlemagne's school?

4. Did the *missi* report to the Emperor?

5. Were Charlemagne's laws called capitularies?

6. Could the conquered tribes keep their own laws?

7. Was Charlemagne a true Roman?

8. Did the Franks overcome the Lombards, Saxons, and Avars?

9. Did Charlemagne drive the Moors out of Spain?

10. Did each count have charge of a district in the Empire?

CHAPTER II

CASTLES, KNIGHTS, AND NOBLES

A new way of living. In Unit Four we read about the fall of the pagan Roman Empire. Unit Five told how Christian civilization was saved from ruin. It showed how the Church became the center of civilization after the fall of Rome.

By degrees the barbarians learned the ways of Christianity and civilization. They began to mix or blend the Latin language with their own. Then, from this mixture, entirely new languages were formed. This was true of many tribes. This was the beginning of such languages as French, Italian, Spanish, and Portuguese. Because they came from the Roman or Latin, they were called Romance languages.

A great ruler arose among the Franks, named Charlemagne. He extended his land until he had almost as much as the former Empire of the West. Because this new Empire was Christian, it was called the Holy Roman Empire. Charlemagne, however, was not a Roman. He was a member of the Frankish tribe.

When Charlemagne died, the great empire began to fall apart. This caused great changes in the way men were governed. Rich nobles began to take over large portions of land. This new system of government and way of life was called the Feudal System. This Chapter tells about the way people lived during this time. Their way of life was very different from ours.

1. Meaning of Feudalism

During the time of the barbarian invasions, the people of Europe were very frightened. They wanted protection from their new enemies. But there was no great ruler to protect them. The barbarians were everywhere.

A battle in the middle ages

The people needed more protection as time went on. Through the Middle Ages there were constant wars among the nobles. Some of these nobles were more powerful than the king. Some of these nobles had strong armies behind them. Others had no way to protect their lands. They looked about for someone to protect their lands.

All the land in a country belonged to the king of that country. To protect his land the king needed a strong army. No king, however, had enough money to pay the men who fought for him. Therefore, he gave away a part of his land to a landowner. He did this on condition that this landowner would provide soldiers to fight for him in time of war. These landowners became nobles. Such a noble was also called the lord of his manor, or estate.

The common people. The noble had a right to govern all the people who lived on his land. These people who worked on the land were the common people, called serfs. When an estate was bought or sold, the serfs went along with it, just as did the buildings and other equipment.

There were many, many serfs in the Middle Ages. They had more rights than slaves, but they were not completely free either.

The duties of the serfs. For three days each week the serfs had to work on the land. On the other days they were allowed to cultivate patches of land for themselves. They had to give even part of what they raised on their own land to their lord also. They had to make special gifts of eggs and chickens to him at Christmas and Easter.

The serfs had to work very hard at other duties also. They had to repair roads and bridges. They hauled stone and lumber for building castles. They ground their corn at the master's mill and baked their bread in his ovens. The wives and daughters of the serfs helped with the housework of the castle or manor house where the lord lived.

The serfs were protected by their lord from attack by other nobles. The army of their lord gave them some security.

The clothing of the serfs was of the very poorest. They lived outside the castle walls, in miserable huts. These huts were often crowded close together on narrow, muddy streets. Whole families of serfs slept together in the same room on a dirt floor covered with straw. The serfs had few pleasures. However, on feast days and Sundays they did not have to work. Then they went to church and often had games and dancing afterwards.

Other workers. Not all the common people lived as serfs. There were some who were better off than the serfs. Among such people were those who worked at trades such as carpentry, milling, and blacksmithing.

There were also the freemen. These people owned their own land. They had to depend upon some neighboring lord to protect them from the raids of other nobles. Usually, they paid the lord for this protection.

2. Ceremony of Homage

The lord or noble sometimes gave part of his land, or estate to another person. This other person was then called a vassal of the lord. When the lord gave away a part of his land, a special ceremony was performed. This ceremony was called *homage* (hom'-aj). It was a very solemn act and one in which the vassal took on new duties.

The vassal would appear at the lord's castle on the appointed day. He would come dressed as if ready for battle, with his armor. He then knelt before his lord and made a solemn oath to be faithful to his new duties as vassal. The lord then accepted his promise, kissed him, and raised him to his feet. Then he put a twig from the land in his hand, or gave him a basin of water from one of the streams on the land, or a lump of soil. This showed that the vassal was now the new ruler and owner of the land.

Duties of the vassal. The vassal promised on his oath to ride to war with his lord. He promised to furnish soldiers for the lord's army and pay the lord sums of money at certain times.

Duties of the lord to the vassal. The lord in turn promised that he would protect his vassal against injury to himself or his property from outside enemies.

When a vassal died his son had the right to inherit the land. He had to give "homage" to the lord who really owned the land.

A medieval castle

3. Castles in the Middle Ages

Every noble had to protect his land from his enemies. These might be other nobles, who were much stronger than he. In building his home, he had to plan it so the enemy could not reach him easily.

First he found a high cliff or an island. On this he built a tall, strong wall for protection. Large round towers were built at the four corners of the wall. Inside the wall he built a castle. This was both a fort and a home for his family.

Outside the high wall there was a drawbridge. Surrounding the wall was a ditch or moat filled with water. One could

Dinner time in a feudal castle

Brown Brothers

cross the moat only by using the bridge. The enemy would have a hard time crossing the moat unless the drawbridge was let down.

Even if the enemy should finally cross the moat, he would find two thick wooden doors that he would have to break open. He would find himself in the first courtyard. In this courtyard were the stables and storehouses.

There was yet another high wall to break down before the second courtyard could be reached. Here was the castle itself, and the keep, where the lord and his family lived. This was a tall building with no windows. This was the last stronghold. When an enemy captured the keep, the castle was completely taken. It was in the lowest floors of the keep that prisoners were held.

Castle life. Castles were dark and damp places. The people usually lived on the upper floors of the castle. There was only one kind of heating system. A large fireplace was built in one corner of the room. Around this fireplace the people of the castle would gather for entertainment. Sometimes a wandering singer or minstrel would appear at the castle and furnish entertainment at close of day. Perhaps the minstrel told stories about Charlemagne's empire or sang the *Song of Roland*. Usually the castle had people called jesters to give merriment and laughter.

4. Steps to Knighthood

The sons of the nobles were not given an education such as boys receive today. They were trained to be ready for war. They were given special training so that they could become knights when they were old enough. Knights were men trained to use arms, such as the sword and spear. They were also trained to be expert horsemen.

The age of knighthood was often called the age of chivalry. Chivalry was the rule of conduct which a true knight was supposed to follow.

The life of a page. A boy of a noble family lived at home until he was about seven years of age. There his mother gave him his first lessons in religion, obedience, and good manners. Then he went to live in the castle of some other noble.

At the noble's castle, the boy began his life as a page. He ran errands, waited on table, and cleaned the armor and weapons of the men. The ladies of the castle taught him to read, write, sing, and play the lyre. The lyre was a musical instrument, like a harp. They also taught him how to behave politely. The page was taught to honor and protect women, to be brave and loyal. The next step to knighthood came when the boy was about fourteen. Then he became a squire.

Life of a squire. The special duty of the squire was to wait upon the lord. He cared for the lord's horses and kept his armor polished. He also learned to handle a shield, spear, and

A knight is made

Culver Service

207

sword. He was taught to ride a horse and to hunt. As he became older he went to battle to fight beside his lord. He took care of his lord if he needed help on the battlefield.

At the age of twenty-one a boy was ready to become a knight. There was a ceremony attached to this great honor.

The ceremony of knighthood. The young squire was given advice on his new life on the day before the ceremony. Then he went to the chapel. There he spent the whole night in prayer, dressed in a simple white garment with long sleeves. Beside him were the weapons and armor which he would receive on the next day.

Early the next morning the squire attended Mass and received Holy Communion. He presented his sword to the priest to bless it. Then he took a solemn oath or promise to defend the Church, respect the priesthood, protect women, and to be faithful to his other duties. His sword was then returned to him.

After Mass the young man knelt before his lord. The lord

William the Conqueror was born in this castle

Brown Brothers

A tournament in the middle ages

drew his own sword and struck the young man on the shoulder. As he did this, he said, "In the name of God, of Our Lady, of thy patron saint, Saint Michael and Saint George, I dub thee knight; be brave, bold, and loyal."

Life of the young knight. The true knight was expected to be gentle, courteous, and faithful to his word.

Often, the knights had contests with other knights. These contests were called tournaments (tur′-na-ments).

In tournaments or in battle the knights wore heavy suits and helmets of metal, called armor. One could not tell one knight from another. The knights began to wear some sign on their armor to let others know who they were. Some wore flowers for a sign, others pictures of an animal or a design. This sign became known as a coat-of-arms for the knights.

Tournaments of the Middle Ages. Usually a king or some rich noble held a tournament. Everyone in the land came, from king to minstrel boy.

Even ladies attended these entertainments.

First, there was a contest between two knights. Such a contest was called a joust (just). Often two large groups of knights took sides against each other, perhaps fifty on each side. Not until most of the knights on one side were unable to fight any longer would the contest end.

Some knights did not live up to their promises made when they were knighted. But many did live as true knights. These men did much to help improve feudal life.

Words We Have Learned

fief	vassal	homage	joust	tournament
drawbridge	serf	manor	armor	keep
chivalry	feudalism	knight	Romance language	

Matching Test

On another paper match Column A with Column B.

Column A
1. vassal
2. serf
3. squire
4. lord
5. knight
6. page

Column B
ruling noble who owned the land
one who was given land by another noble
laborer who belonged to the manor
one trained to be loyal, brave, courteous
the first stage in becoming a knight
one whose duty is to wait upon his lord

Fill the Blanks

1. The ceremony by which a vassal receive land from his lord was called ——————.
2. The land which a lord owned was called a ——————.
3. People who worked on the land of a noble were called —————— .
4. Usually a moat surrounded a castle for —————— during time of war.
5. A sham battle between knights was held at a ——————.
6. The place where the prisoners were held was in the lower part of the —————— .
7. Knights were bound by a code of conduct called ——————.

For Discussion

1. Why were many castles built on a cliff or island?
2. How did the ceremony of homage take place?
3. Compare homage and the ceremony of knighthood.

CHAPTER III

FEUDALISM ON THE CONTINENT

Trouble ahead in Europe. You have been reading about life in Europe during the Middle Ages. You must remember that very few of the people of Europe were rich nobles. The remainder were the common people and clergy. Most of the people were, usually, very poor.

This system of feudalism began around the time of Charlemagne. It got a firm hold in the Holy Roman Empire. You will understand this much better after you have read about feudalism in this chapter.

1. The Empire Is Divided

Charlemagne was a great leader. He fought many wars, and he conquered all his enemies but the Moors in Spain. He was really the first great leader in Europe since the fall of Rome. He was a leader who arose from among the tribes outside the Roman Empire.

The great empire of Charlemagne lasted only during his lifetime. At his death there was no one to carry on his work. No one but Charlemagne could rule so large an empire well.

Charlemagne's son tried to rule the empire. Then when he died his three sons quarreled about the various lands of the Empire. Finally, they came to an agreement. This agreement was called the Treaty of Verdun.

In this treaty the land was divided among the three grandsons of Charlemagne. One of these, named Charles the Bald, was given the western part of the empire, or West Frankland. Louis, another grandson, received the eastern part, or East Frankland. Lothaire received the strip of land in the center and the land now called Italy.

What happened to the land after this? First, we shall see what Charles the Bald did about West Frankland.

This model shows what a Viking ship was like

Charles the Bald was a very weak king. The people did not have confidence in him.

When Charles became king of West Frankland, another great invasion was starting. Another tribe was attacking the land of the Franks.

This tribe was called Vikings or Norsemen. They lived in the north. They had not enough room on their own lands for all of them to live. So they started to make war on the Franks.

The second enemy of Frankland was the Moors. They were threatening the Franks too.

Besides this, Charles the Bald was still having trouble with his brothers over the division of the Empire.

A land without a strong leader. With so many enemies on all sides, the people of West Frankland expected help from their king and his government. But no help and no protection was given to them. What could they do in order to fight the Norsemen and the Moors?

The people looked about for protection. They found a way out. That way was feudalism. Can you tell how feudalism protected the people's rights?

The strong bond increases. As time went on, feudalism grew stronger in West Frankland. After some time, West Frankland came to be called France. The king had no great army, but the nobles had their own armies. They had the armies of their vassals which they could depend upon to help them in time of war. Who, then, was becoming the stronger, the king or the nobles? The nobles, you may be sure. For the nobles had armies to protect them from danger.

Not one of the kings who succeeded Charles became powerful. Each was a king merely in name. He did not rule his land. The nobles really ruled France at this time.

There was almost constant warfare going on in France. When a noble was not fighting another noble, he was keeping the Norsemen from his land, or perhaps the Moors.

2. The Church Tries to Keep Peace

During the time of feudal wars, the Church took steps to help the people. The Church wanted men to live peacefully. But the Church could not take sides in these wars. The Church, however, did much to prevent and stop the wars.

The Truce of God. First, the Church made a rule that no fighting was to take place from Thursday night until Monday morning of each week. This rule forbade fighting in Lent and Advent, and on great feast-days of the Church. This rule was called the Truce of God.

As time went on, the Church added other days to the time when fighting was forbidden. Fighting was forbidden during harvest time. This especially helped the serfs. Very often their harvests had been ruined by the armies of nobles who had trampled upon them on their way to battle.

Peace of God. The Church also forbade fighting to take place around holy places, such as monasteries and churches. Knights were forbidden to attack serfs, pilgrims, or merchants. This rule was called the Peace of God.

Almost all Europe was Christian during the days of feudalism. These laws made by the Church were for all Christians. The Christians had to obey them. If a noble would dare to disobey these laws, the Church could punish him. The Church would not allow the noble to receive the sacraments of the

Church. This terrible penance was called interdict.

The Church made these laws for the good of the people. The Church always guides the people in the ways of peace, charity and justice.

One enemy satisfied. After the death of Charles the Bald, other kings who were descended from Charlemagne ruled the land known as France. We call these kings Carolingian kings, after the word for Charles.

Still the Vikings continued their attacks. They attacked especially the western coast of Europe. On the way they robbed many churches and destroyed works of art in monasteries.

One king named Charles the Simple found a way of keeping the peace. He made Rolf, the head of the Norsemen, his vassal. He gave him part of his land in the north of France. Here the Norsemen settled down. This land became known as Normandy. After awhile these Norsemen became civilized and began to live just as their neighbors, the French, did.

Now one of the rich nobles who fought very hard to keep out the Vikings from France was named Odo. Odo was Count of Paris in 887. Odo became very popular and famous in France.

The king at this time was Charles the Fat. The nobles did not like him. They took the throne away from him and made Odo the king of France.

This was the end of the Carolingian kings. For the past hundred years Charlemagne and his descendants had ruled this land called France. Now Odo was king. He was not related to Charlemagne at all.

When Odo died, the nobles of France elected a king. The one whom they chose was a rich and powerful duke named Hugh Capet (ka-pay'). He owned very much land and many nobles had to pay him homage. Still others were related to him in some way.

Hugh Capet became king of France in 987 A.D. From that time until 1328 all the kings of France were descended from Hugh Capet. That is, they belonged to the Capetian (ka-pee'-shen) line of kings.

3. Three Famous Kings

Kings who did not rule. By this time, feudalism was in full swing in France. There were nineteen different nobles who

This old French town is still surrounded by walls and towers

owned the land of France. Only one section of France was owned directly by the king of France.

Each of these nobles made his own laws for his own land. The nobles did the ruling while the king did very little about uniting France. It was the day of triumph for the nobles.

However, during the period from 987 to 1328, there were a few strong kings in France. Four of them are worth mentioning. One of them is a saint. Is it easy for a king to become a saint?

Regaining the land. In 1180, Philip Augustus was king of France. Even the king of England was one of his vassals.

Philip Augustus did all he could to weaken the power of the nobles. He made them pay taxes. He encouraged the serfs to make their living by trade, not by farming. He helped the serfs to build towns. He even granted them charters, with certain rights and privileges. He believed he could rely on the serfs more than the nobles.

Do you think he was right? We shall see.

King Louis, the Saint. Louis IX of France was one of the strong Capetian kings. His mother, Saint Blanche, was a very pious woman. She taught her son to love and serve God above all other things in this world. She prayed hard that her son would never offend the good God by committing a mortal sin.

God always hears the prayers of those who want to serve Him well. Saint Louis lived a holy life, even as a king. He did many acts of kindness for sick people, the poor, and lepers. He did away with the horrible practice of deciding matters by a duel. He forbade also other unfair methods of trial.

King Saint Louis died while on a Crusade. You will read about this later in this book.

Three classes of people. King Saint Louis had a grandson who was very handsome. People called him Philip the Fair. When he became king he made everyone in the kingdom pay taxes to help support his kingdom.

About this time in France there arose three classes of people. These classes were called Estates. The priests and bishops were members of the First Estate. The nobles belonged to the Second Estate. The Third Estate was composed of the common people, who were now beginning to live in towns, rather than in villages as serfs.

Philip called a meeting of these three classes of people. At the meeting they discussed taxes. This meeting was called the Estates General. However, no king ever called a meeting of the Estates General for many years after that.

You will understand from what you have just read that it took France many, many years before it could break the strength of feudalism and become a nation.

4. Early Rulers of Germany

Of all Charlemagne's grandsons, Louis the German was the best ruler. The Northmen were bothering him, too, as well as his brother in France. Besides, Louis had other tribes invading his lands on the east and southeast.

These invaders were not Teutons. They were Slavs and Hungarians.

The Slavs were from central Russia. By degrees they took over lands to the west of them. Whenever other tribes left land vacant and went farther westward, the Slavs moved onto this land. In time, they came to hold all the land in the east of Europe.

Slavs become Christians. It is interesting to know how the Gospel of Christ was first preached to these Slavs. There were in Constantinople two brothers named Cyril and Methodius. These were Christians, of Slavic descent. They obtained permission to preach the true Christian religion to the Slavs in the north.

Saint Cyril wanted very much to teach the Slavs about the Bible and ceremonies of the Church. But the Slavs had no written language of their own. So Saint Cyril invented an alphabet for them. That alphabet is still used in some Slavic languages, except for a few changes. Slavic priests still celebrate Holy Mass in their own language.

After this, many of the Slavs were converted. The King of Bulgaria and his people became Christians. Since Saints Cyril and Methodius came from Constantinople, these people were joined to the Church under the patriarch, or leading bishop, of Constantinople.

5. Emperor of Germany and Italy

Germany did not have Caro-lingian kings for long. In 911, a Saxon king, Conrad, took over the throne of Germany. Seven years later, Henry the Fowler became strong enough to gain the throne. The nobles liked Henry the Fowler very much.

On the death of Henry, his son, Otto I, was elected king. Otto conquered Italy. Italy, you know, was given to Lothaire at the Treaty of Verdun. But he did not keep it long. It had now become part of the land owned by the German Emperor.

The kingdom ruled by Otto I was still land owned by nobles. It was not one large country ruled by a king. Rather it was land owned by several nobles, each like a little king ruling his own property.

At Rome, Otto I was crowned by the Pope as head of the Holy Roman Empire.

Was this like Charlemagne's empire? In 800, Charlemagne first received the title of Holy Roman Emperor. Then France, Germany, and Italy were part of his great kingdom. Otto I had for an empire Germany and Italy. It was really an empire *only in name.* The land was divided into several sections and ruled by nobles.

Charlemagne lived in West

Frankland. Otto lived in Germany. Charlemagne's empire lasted during his reign of forty years and then fell to ruin. Otto's empire existed more than eight hundred years afterward.

Things went on in Germany for many years, as they did in France. Feudalism was controlled by the nobles. But the Holy Roman Empire of Germany never became a strong empire. Soon towns grew up along the trade routes. More and more people began to leave the farms and manors and move into these towns. Since more workers were moving away, it became harder to operate the large estates. The rule of lords and nobles was weakened. This meant feudalism was declining.

As a result of these changes, Italy broke away from the control of Germany. Still, it took many years before Italy developed as a nation. You will learn more about this topic later, in another Unit.

For a time there was no emperor at all in Germany. Then a member of the Hapsburg family was chosen emperor. This king built up a part of Germany which later became the country of Austria.

Keeping Up with Our Vocabulary

interdict   Peace of God   Truce of God   estates

Things to Talk About

1. Why was Charlemagne's Empire different from Otto's Holy Roman Empire?
2. If you had lived in 962 A.D. where would you have liked to have been on Christmas Day?

Mastery in Matching

On another paper, match Column A with Column B.

Column A

1. Saint Cyril
2. Saint Louis
3. Hugh Capet
4. Otto I
5. Louis the German

Column B

one of Charlemagne's grandsons
Count of Paris who became King of France
one of the Capetian kings
the composer of the Slavic alphabet
crowned Holy Roman Emperor in 962

CHAPTER IV

BEFORE THE NORMANS CAME TO ENGLAND

Invasions of England. You have learned that the Franks were the first barbarians to become Christians. They also founded a large Empire which was called the Holy Roman Empire. Later this Empire was divided, and the two nations of France and Germany began their existence.

Another nation was soon to arise. That nation was England. England, in the early days, was called Britain. One after another, various tribes conquered and settled upon that island. After some years, they became part of the culture and pattern of the country. England was one of the first nations to arise as a result of the wanderings of the various tribes.

This chapter tells how England became important. It points out that, at a very early date, the common people in England were given rights and privileges unheard of in France or Germany.

It is good for us Americans to remember the story of early England. All freedom comes to us from God. But it was the people of England who helped bring this freedom to America. Freedom has always been dear to the English.

1. Land of Invasions

Romans in Britain. After Caesar conquered Britain, other Romans came and ruled it. These Romans came a hundred years after Caesar. They were Christians. They stayed there for about three hundred and fifty years. Best of all, they brought the Christian religion to Britain. The Britons, as the people were called, became civilized because of this invasion.

While in Britain, the Romans built a great wall between them and the enemy tribes in the

This old bridge was built by the Romans. It still stands in England

north. Parts of this wall are still standing.

You remember that Rome was attacked by the Goths. When this happened, the Roman soldiers were recalled to Rome to fight their enemies there. This was the end of the Roman government of Britain. **Britons need help.** Britain went to pieces after that. The terrible enemies in the north swept down upon Britons. These enemies destroyed British towns and made slaves of the people.

Now, on the continent of Europe, in the north, there lived some tribes called Angles, Saxons, and Jutes. The Britons invited the Jutes to help them fight the Picts and Scots.

The Britons flee for their lives. The Jutes did a fine work for the Britons and defeated the Picts. But the Jutes became fond of Britain, too. They refused to go back to their former homes on the continent. To make matters worse, the Angles and Saxons came over to Britain and settled down.

Now it was the Britons against the Jutes. The Jutes

won. The Britons were obliged to leave their dearly loved homes. Some went to Europe. Others made their homes in Wales.

2. When England Was Angle-Land

The Christian religion died out in Britain when the Britons were scattered. The Angles divided the land among them until there were seven little kingdoms there. The land became known as Angle-land, and soon afterwards, England.

In an earlier Unit of this text, you read about Saint Augustine. It was he who came from Rome to convert the Angles and Saxons. Saint Augustine went to the little kingdom in the south, called Kent. He lived at its chief city, Canterbury. Once again, the Christian faith was brought to England. The Irish monks from Iona and Lindisfarne also helped to spread the religion in parts of England.

Wessex wins. But the seven kingdoms of England did not get along well. They were continually fighting with one another. At one time Kent was the leading kingdom. Finally, Wessex conquered all the others. Then England was united for the first time in Anglo-Saxon days. This was about 828 A.D.

Can you guess why Wessex was the winner in this? Wessex had at that time a strong leader, a prince named Egbert. Egbert had at one time been in the court of Charlemagne. He recalled how Charlemagne ruled the people there. He tried to make wise and fair laws for his people as Charlemagne did.

Egbert did not have peace very long. The Norsemen, who plundered during the reign of Charlemagne, started attacking towns on the coast of England. Some of these Norsemen came from Denmark, so the people of England called them Danes.

The Danes conquered a strip of land in the east of England. It looked bad for the Angles and Saxons, until Egbert's grandson became king. This young king's name was Alfred. He was so fine a king that he was called "Alfred the Great."

3. Rule of King Alfred the Great

King Alfred was determined not to let the Danes conquer England. He fought and fought, but the Danes kept on fighting, too. King Alfred found a way out of his trouble. He made a treaty with the Danes. He gave them a strip of land they had already conquered. This land was called Danelaw (dane'-law).

The Danes promised to stay on this land and not disturb any other part of the country. Of course, they had to recognize Alfred as their king.

As time went on, the Danes became more and more like the other people in England. Their ways of living, language, and laws soon became like those of the Anglo-Saxons.

Ruling England. King Alfred knew that England needed a strong navy. He established one that was very efficient.

He also established law courts in England. The people elected officers for these courts, called sheriffs. Alfred called together some wise men of the kingdom, and made them his Council. This Council which gave the king advice was called the *Witan* (wit'-an).

Education during Alfred's reign. Alfred did not receive much schooling when he was young. Still, he studied Latin and was able to read Latin books. He wanted his people to be edu-

King Alfred visiting a monastery school

cated. For this purpose, he founded a palace school of his own at Winchester.

Alfred wrote a book on the early history of England. It told how people lived in England in early days. This book was called the *Anglo-Saxon Chronicle*. Because of this, Alfred has been called the Father of English Literature.

Of course, the English that Alfred spoke was not exactly like the English which you speak today.

England, land of Mary. Alfred was a good Catholic. He built monasteries and gave much money towards the building of churches and monasteries in England. In fact, all England was Christian in belief at that time. It was lovingly called "Mary's Dowry," or "the land that belongs to Mary."

When Alfred's great-grandson, Edgar, became king, he was crowned by the Archbishop of Canterbury. King Edgar was able to rule England as one large kingdom, for the Danes had the same laws and customs as the Anglo-Saxons.

Canterbury Cathedral. This shows the Norman Style of architecture

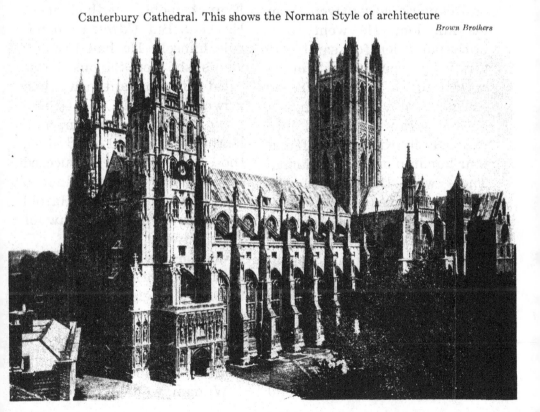

After a hundred years. The Danes in Europe began moving again. This time they were well organized. They had already won Denmark, Norway, and Sweden. In 1016, their powerful king, named Canute (kanoot') conquered England. Canute was a wise and just leader. He did all he could to help the people.

The Danes who attacked England this time were Christians. These Danes had became Christians due to one of their kings, named Harold.

In the year 826, King Harold of Denmark was driven from his kingdom. He went to a Christian ruler for safety. If this ruler would help him he agreed to be baptized. Saint Ansgar, a holy priest who was born in France, received into the Church King Harold and four hundred of the Northmen. These were the first of the northern peoples to be baptized.

After that, Saint Ansgar spent thirty-eight years as a missionary, working among the Norsemen. He is called the Apostle of the North. He died in 865.

4. The Norman Victory

Who shall be king? After the death of Canute, there was no strong leader to succeed him. In 1042, a grandson of King Edgar came to the throne. He was called Edward the Confessor. He was called "the Confessor" because he was a very pious man.

Now Edward's mother was a Norman, that is, she was from Normandy, on the continent. Edward had grown up in Normandy. So Edward spoke French, like the people in France. He was the first king of England to come from Normandy.

Edward brought some French nobles with him to England. But Edward did not rule himself. He had two advisors who were Saxons. These ruled with more authority than Edward himself. One of these Saxon nobles was named Harold. When Edward died, there was no one to succeed him. So the nobles elected Harold as their king. Harold was also a brother-in-law of King Edward.

Rivals for the throne. William, a duke in Normandy, said the throne of England belonged to him. He was really a cousin of King Edward. He claimed also that Edward promised the English throne to him.

William wanted the throne

of England very much. He gathered a large army and sailed across the English Channel. The forces of William landed near London, at a place called Hastings. There he fought the army of Harold. Both sides fought very hard. But the Normans were better prepared to fight. In the battle, Harold was killed. The Normans won. It was the year 1066.

William went to London where he received the crown. From that time on, William was known as William the Conqueror.

New Words to Study

Anglo-Saxon Chronicle   sheriff   Witan

A Little Play

The name of your play will be "People who invaded England." One group will be Romans, another Jutes, another Angles and Saxons, and the last group Danes and Normans. Each pupil will write three sentences about the tribe which his group represents. Here are some questions to help you.

1. What tribe was the first to receive Christianity after the Romans left Britain?

2. To which tribe did Alfred belong? Canute? Saint Boniface? Harold? William I?

3. England is named after which tribe?

4. Which tribe is called Danes in England, and another name in Normandy?

Fill in This Chart on Another Paper

Name of Leader	Tribe	Name of Country Ruled	Religion	Early Education of Leader
Alfred the Great	-----------	---------------	---------------	-------------------
Charlemagne	-----------	---------------	---------------	-------------------

CHAPTER V

LIBERTY UNDER THE MAGNA CARTA

England, a changed country. After William the Conqueror had won the throne of England, a great change came over that country. William brought Norman nobles to England with him. He spoke French, lived like the French, and dressed like the French.

The Anglo-Saxons still spoke their own language, while the people of the court spoke French. In time, however, French words came into the Anglo-Saxon language. Even our English language today contains Anglo-Saxon words and French words. There also are some words which come from Latin and other languages.

But William's victory meant more than changes in language. For one thing, it gave more power to the people in England.

The great English document, called the Magna Carta, or Great Charter, was written during this period. Later, the English colonists brought to America their love for liberty. This love of liberty is what caused the Magna Carta to be drawn up.

1. Rule of William the Conqueror

William wanted to be a strong king. He gave the rich lands to his friends, the Norman barons. But he did not give them large estates all in one place. He gave them lands in various parts of the kingdom.

Feudalism in England. The next thing William did was to make every noble take an oath of loyalty to him. They had to promise to defend the king at all times. This is what made English feudalism different from feudalism on the continent. In France and Germany the vassal made an oath of loyalty to his lord. But in England the vassals and lords made an oath of loyalty to William I, the King of England. Do you think this helped to make William a strong king?

William was a stern man. He kept good order everywhere. He was mild to men who served God and very severe to those who were not obedient and just.

William wanted to keep an account of all the property in England and who owned it. He therefore had a book made in which was kept the record of all the people and property in the kingdom. This book was called the *Domesday Book*.

What the Normans did for England. The Normans brought many good things to England. Architects and masons came. These men taught the English how to build with stone in place of wood. They built many beautiful Norman castles and churches.

The language of the English court became French. The English learned French ways of living and the use of French weapons.

2. Henry II Restores Order

When William the Conqueror

This is part of the Domesday Book

William the Conqueror

died in 1087, the people of England were sad indeed. They knew that his sons did not have his ability to rule.

For about a hundred years, there was no one to check the growing power of the nobles. They built many castles and fought with other nobles. Sometimes the country seemed to have no government at all. It was almost as dreadful as the invasion of the Danes had been.

Then a powerful king came to the throne. His mother was a granddaughter of William the Conqueror. His father was French also. This new king was Henry II. Not only was he king of England. He was lord of half of France.

Henry saw what England needed at that time. He knew how to bring order and justice to the country.

For twenty years England had been having civil war. Though Henry could fight well, he did not like war. Therefore, he forbade the Norman barons to do any more fighting. He destroyed their castles and broke up their armies. England was at peace again.

3. Henry II and Common Law

One of the most important things Henry did was to change the methods of trial in England. Before his time, the usual way of finding out if an accused person was guilty, was by the ordeal.

Sometimes these ordeals were battles between two persons suspected of being guilty. Each was given a weapon with which to fight. The defeated party was supposed to be guilty.

The people had a very wrong idea of how to judge a man. They thought that, if a man were innocent, God would allow him to win the fight. They were wrong about this. God expects people to practice justice and he gave them reason to discover what is fair and just. That is the wise and intelligent way to act. It is wrong to expect God to perform a miracle when people do not act according to reason.

What Henry planned to do. King Henry planned another kind of trial. First he had many intelligent men trained as judges in his court. Then he sent them to all the chief cities. They carried out justice in the same manner everywhere they went. Anyone who had been accused of a crime was brought before them. They asked witnesses to tell what had happened. If this jury saw there was good reason to believe the accused was guilty, he was brought before a judge for trial.

When one of these judges would arrive in a city, twelve worthy men were chosen to work with him. These men were later called the grand jury.

This was not all. Twelve other men of the neighborhood attended the trial. They listened to the trial and heard all the sides of each story, or case. After the trial was over, these twelve men decided whether or not the person accused had broken the law. This was called

A medieval trial

"trial by jury." Why do you think this was a just way of deciding whether one was guilty or innocent? Do we have trial by jury in our country today?

The Common Law of England. As time went on, the judges and jury followed the same just manner of carrying on trials. They tried to act justly in each particular case. They followed rules which were reasonable and the same for all. Even though these rules were not written down, they were real laws. Everybody knew what these rules were. That is why these laws were known as Common Law. By 1600, common law was well established. When English people came to America, they brought with them the love and practice of common law.

A Saint of the Church. King Henry II was a powerful king with lands in both France and England. But he went too far and interfered with the laws of the Church. He thought he could make the Church obey him.

At that time, the Archbishop of Canterbury was a holy man named Thomas a Becket. Although he knew that the King would not like it, he told the King that he could not interfere with the Church. The Church must be free, Thomas said, to do the work of God.

This made the King angry. One day, in the presence of some of his knights, the King said he wished Thomas a Becket were out of his way.

Shortly after that, Thomas a Becket was at the altar in the Cathedral of Canterbury. Some of the King's knights entered the church, approached the altar, and murdered Thomas on the spot.

Everyone in London was shocked at this cruelty and injustice. King Henry, too, was sorry. He did penance for his

Brown Brothers
Death of Saint Thomas a Becket

sin. He restored to the Church at Canterbury the property he had taken for himself.

In three years Saint Thomas a Becket was canonized as a saint and martyr. Every year after that, the English people used to make pilgrimages to the tomb of Saint Thomas a Becket. You will later read stories about these pilgrimages in a famous story called the *Canterbury Tales.*

King Henry II had two sons, Richard and John. Richard succeeded him on the throne. King Richard spent most of his time away from England on a Crusade. You will read about this Crusade later.

4. John a Cruel King and Tyrant

The rule of a tyrant. William the Conqueror and Henry II sometimes made mistakes, yet in general they were good kings. They tried to be just. However, King John, son of Henry II, was not like his father. He was a tyrant and had no mercy for anyone. He even had his own nephew shamefully killed. No king after him ever was given the name of John because of this tyrant's reputation.

King John loses land in France. Ever since William the Conqueror had become King of England, Normandy also belonged to the King of England. Now King John did not govern Normandy as he should. Therefore the King of France led his army against John. He was disgracefully defeated and lost all his possessions in Normandy. The French king who now owned Normandy was Philip Augustus, about whom you read in Chapter III.

A quarrel with the Pope. King John made another big mistake. Pope Innocent III had appointed Stephen Langton the new Archbishop of Canterbury. Stephen Langton was already a Cardinal, and had been many years in Rome before the Pope sent him to England. King John did not like the appointment of Stephen Langton. He would not allow Stephen Langton to land on English soil. The tyrant king wanted to appoint the new archbishop himself. You know that the Pope has the power to appoint bishops and archbishops in the Church in all parts of the world. But King John was a stubborn man. He refused to accept Cardinal Langton. The Pope and many bishops tried their best to make John see his error.

King John is punished. The Church has a special punishment for people who do great wrong. Pope Innocent III had to punish John. The punishment is called an interdict. This meant that every church in England was closed. No church bells were allowed to be rung. No priests were allowed to preach. No sacraments could be given, except Baptism for infants. The English people were very unhappy over this. Yet the king only laughed at them when they complained about this state of affairs.

Finally, the King had to give in. He said he would make peace with the Pope. Stephen Langton was permitted to be archbishop and the interdict was taken off the country.

Unhappiness continues. John continued after that to be very cruel to his own people. England was an unhappy place. People were wrongfully imprisoned by the king and his officers. Money, goods, and lands were taken away from the people for no reason at all.

The English people have a legend about a leader at this time who tried to right the wrongs done to the people. His name was Robin Hood. The people loved Robin Hood, but the king's men were afraid of him. Have you ever read stories of King John's men and Robin Hood?

Preparing the Charter. Things went from bad to worse in England. The barons and people were becoming more discontented every day. They had to pay enormous taxes to the king.

Something had to be done to put a stop to the king's unjust manner of ruling everyone. The barons and the churchmen, headed by Stephen Langton, wrote out a document. This

This shows part of the Magna Carta

document listed the rights they wanted the king to give them. Altogether the document had sixty-three points.

These rights, you know, are those which have been given to every man by God. But King John had not given these rights to his subjects.

There were rights listed in the document for the nobles and lords, for the Church, and English people in general.

Three very important points were:

1. No person could be held in prison without trial.
2. Justice and rights could neither be sold nor denied to anyone.
3. The people could be forced to pay only the taxes required by the Great Council of the Nation.

5. The Signing of the Magna Carta

This great document was called the Great Charter. Some people like better its Latin name, *Magna Carta.*

One June day in 1215, a large group of knights, barons, and common people met King John in a field called Runnymede. One of the group spoke for the others. He said the king must sign the charter. The king saw that the barons were very

Brown Brothers
King John signs the Great Charter

angry. He began to fear what they might do to him. King John signed the Great Charter. This was a very important step in freedom for the people. It was June 15, 1215.

Next Stephen Langton and the barons signed the Great Charter and attached their seals.

Foundation of English liberty. No wonder that Englishmen through the years have loved the Great Charter. When some kings tried to break the Charter, the people always reminded them of their rights. The truths contained in the Great Charter protected the freedom of the people. Freedom is one of God's gifts to us. Would you call Cardinal Stephen Langton one of the Founders of Freedom? If so, why?

All Englishmen know that the Great Charter is the foundation of English liberty. Even when Englishmen came to America they expected the king of England to give them the rights in the Great Charter. When King George III tried to take these rights from them they rebelled. They wrote their reasons in the Declaration of Independence. That is why we say that our rights come down from the Great Charter. Many of these rights were written in our Constitution by our Founding Fathers.

King John rejects the Charter. King John did not keep his word. He refused the people their rights. However, he died soon afterward and his son Henry III, followed in his footsteps. Henry was no better than his father.

The nobles got together, made him a prisoner, and ruled the country themselves, headed by a noble named Simon de Montfort. They changed the Great Council of barons, who advised the king. They made it possible for the common people

Brown Brothers

King John's seal

to be represented. Two men from each town and two men from each county came to the meeting with the nobles and bishops. This was the first Parliament. It was the first time the common people had a chance to speak about affairs which concerned them in the government.

When King Edward the First came into power, he made another important change in the Parliament. He divided it into two parts, or houses. The House of Lords was for nobles and churchmen. The House of Commons was made up of men chosen by the common people. Sometimes Edward's Parliament is called the "Model Parliament." Can you tell why?

For Discussion

1. What is meant by the Norman Conquest?
2. How did the Great Charter protect English liberty?
3. Why was trial by ordeal un-

just?
4. Why does the name of Saint Thomas a Becket stand for one who lives by the law of God?

Words to Learn

Parliament
ordeal
trial by jury

Great Charter
Domesday Book

Multiple Choice

1. The last peoples to invade England were the
   a. Danes
   b. Anglo-Saxons
   c. Normans
   d. Celts
2. The King who signed the Great Charter was
   a. Henry II
   b. John
   c. Richard the Lionhearted
   d. Alfred the Great
3. The Archbishop of Canterbury who helped the people get their rights was
   a. Saint Thomas a Becket
   b. Stephen Langton
   c. Saint Boniface
   d. Saint Augustine
4. The rights of the nobles, churchmen, and people were written in the
   a. the Domesday Book
   b. the Anglo-Saxon Chronicle
   c. Canterbury Tales
   d. Great Charter
5. Trial by jury was begun dur-

ing the reign of
   a. Alfred the Great
   b. Henry III
   c. John
   d. Henry II
6. The punishment called interdict was placed upon England by
   a. Pope Innocent III
   b. Philip Augustus of France
   c. Stephen Langton
   d. Saint Thomas a Becket
7. Harold was defeated by William the Conqueror at the battle of
   a. Runnymede
   b. Hastings
   c. Tours
   d. London
8. The change made by William the Conqueror in bringing feudalism to England was
   a. the nobles were given more power to rule their own lands
   b. the French nobles could not live in castles

c. every vassal had to swear allegiance first to the king
d. there were no longer any vassals, just barons and nobles of England

9. The King who lost his French possession to the French King was
   a. Henry II
   b. William I
   c. John
   d. Richard

10. The great document of English liberty is called
    a. The Constitution
    b. The Great Council
    c. the Great Charter
    d. Domesday Book

Things to Do

1. The English called their law-making body Parliament. Find out what the United States calls its law-making body in Washington.
2. Does the United States have two houses where laws are discussed? Name them.
3. Find on your map the country of Normandy. Tell on your paper why it was called by this name; why people in England began to speak French in 1066.
4. Write four sentences explaining the Great Charter, telling why it was important.
5. Find on your map the lands owned by Charlemagne. Show how the empire was divided by the Treaty of Verdun.
6. Tell the difference between the pagan Roman Empire and the Holy Roman Empire of Charlemagne. Show the lands contained in each. Was the Holy Roman Empire of Otto I the same land as that of Charlemagne's Empire?
7. Find stories of King Alfred the Great in your school or city library. Also stories of King Canute, Robin Hood, Saint Thomas a Becket, Saints Cyril and Methodius.
8. Tell why it was a good thing for England to have been conquered by William of Normandy.

Highlights of This Unit

1. The freedom we enjoy in America today had its beginnings in the Old World.
2. The first barbarian kingdom to become Christian was that of Clovis, the Frankish King, husband of Clotilda.
3. Pepin fought the Lombards

and gave the lands gained to the Pope.

4. Charles Martel defeated the Mohammedans at the Battle of Tours in 732 A.D.
5. Charlemagne was crowned ruler of the Holy Roman Empire in the West in 800 A.D.
6. After the death of Charlemagne, his kingdom was divided by the Treaty of Verdun.
7. There was no strong king to protect the people from invasions, so a new way of life began, called feudalism.
8. Feudalism reigned through early France and Germany because no king was strong enough to break the power of the nobles.
9. In Germany, a king named Otto I had Germany and Italy as his empire. He was crowned by the Pope as Holy Roman Emperor in 962 A.D.
10. Angles and Saxons destroyed the early Roman civilization in England.
11. Alfred the Great saved England from the Danes.
12. William the Conqueror defeated the English at Hastings in 1066.
13. Archbishop Stephen Langton, with the aid of the barons, drew up the Great Charter of English liberties in 1215.
14. Henry II developed a system of trial by jury and gave the world the Common Law which has come down to us today.
15. The nobles under Simon de Montfort met together at the first Parliament in 1265.
16. In 1295 Parliament was divided into the House of Lords and House of Commons.
17. Saint Ansgar is called the Apostle of the North.

Mastery Test on Unit Six

I. Choose the correct word or words to complete the following sentences.

Mohammedanism   homage
Anglo-Saxon Chronicle   oath
Normandy

English language   palace school
Great Charter   Canterbury
trial by jury   Tales

1. Charles Martel stopped the spread of _____ in Europe.
2. Henry II introduced into England the system of _____.
3. Alcuin taught at the _____ owned by Charlemagne.
4. Saint Thomas a Becket's

shrine was visited by pilgrims in the ―――――.

5. William I of England made every noble take an ――――― to serve him.

6. The Normans added new words and phrases to the ―――――.

7. King John was forced to sign the ――――― in 1215.

8. The story of early England is found in the ――――― of Alfred the Great.

9. Land given by the French king to the Northmen was called ―――――.

10. The oath of allegiance given to a vassal by an overlord is called ―――――.

II. Match Column A with Column B. Write complete sentences on your paper.

Column A	*Column B*
1. Charlemagne	a. Christian wife of the Frankish king
2. Pepin	b. baptized by Saint Remigius
3. Clovis	c. Apostles who converted the Slavs
4. Edward the Confessor	d. an English king
5. Clotilda	e. gave lands in Italy to the Pope
6. Saints Cyril and Methodius	f. crowned king of Holy Roman Empire in 800 A.D.
7. Otto I	g. crowned Holy Roman Emperor in 962 A.D.

III. Answer the following questions by one word on your paper.

1. What was the Council of Alfred the Great called?

2. What did Simon de Montfort call his council?

3. What religious group did Charles Martel defeat?

4. Which Archbishop of Canterbury was not allowed to enter England at first but was later admitted?

5. What country did the Capetian Kings rule?

6. Which grandson of Charlemagne was given lands called Germany?

7. Which Holy Roman Emperor had Germany and Italy only in his Empire?

8. Which French King took Normandy and other French lands away from John?

9. What is the name of the lands Alfred gave to the Danes?

10. What language mixed with the Anglo-Saxon to form the English language?

IV. Answer the following by "Yes" or "No."

1. Was Harold defeated by William at the battle of Hastings?
2. Did Charles Martel defeat the Mohammedans at Runnymede?
3. Was Saint Thomas a Becket martyred at Rome?
4. Did Saint Cyril invent an alphabet for the Slavs?
5. Did William the Conqueror write the Anglo-Saxon Chronicle?
6. Was a vassal one who received land from a noble in return for services in time of war?
7. Was the Treaty of Verdun made by Alfred the Great?
8. Was Canute a Danish king who ruled England also?
9. Was France part of the Holy Roman Empire under Otto I?
10. Was France ruled by weak kings after the death of Charlemagne?
11. Were the Romans the first to invade Britain?

V. Arrange the following in the order in which they happened.

1. Charlemagne crowned Emperor
2. Treaty of Verdun
3. Hugh Capet made king of France
4. Otto I crowned Emperor
5. Fall of the Roman Empire (pagan)

Do the same with the following:

1. The Great Charter is signed
2. The Battle of Hastings took place
3. The first English Parliament met in session
4. The Battle of Tours took place
5. The Danes invade England the second time

VI. Answer the following in complete sentences.

1. How did Charlemagne show he was interested in learning?
2. How did Alfred the Great help people to get an education?
3. Why is the Battle of Hastings important in the history of England?
4. What was the difference between feudalism in England and that on the continent?

239

Hymns to Mary

HISTORY OF HYMNS. From early times, Catholics honored God by holding processions. One of the earliest hymns for processions is "Vexilla Regis." It was written by Vincentius Fortunatus to be sung during the procession which brought the relic of the True Cross from Tours to Poitiers in 569, it is still sung on Good Friday. Another processional hymn of Holy Week is the "Gloria, Laus." If possible this hymn is sung by a children's choir, in imitation of the children who sang to Our Lord on Palm Sunday. St. Theodolph, Bishop of Orleans (c.760–821) composed this hymn.

ORIGIN AND MEANING. St. Alphonsus, the author of "Look Down, O Mother Mary," was noted for his devotion to the Blessed Virgin. One of the most famous books ever written about Mary, "The Glories of Mary," was written by St. Alphonsus, and this hymn appears in it. This hymn is one of the most popular by St. Alphonsus in honor of Mary.

Look Down, O Mother Mary!

Look down, O Mother Mary
   From thy bright throne above;
Cast down upon thy children
   One only glance of love.

And if a heart so tender
   With pity flows not o'er,
Then turn away, O Mother!
   And look on us no more.

See how, ungrateful sinners,
   We stand before thy Son;
His loving Heart upbraids us
   The evil we have done.

But if thou wilt appease Him,
   Speak for us,—but one word;
Thou only can'st obtain us
   The pardon of our Lord.

O Mary, dearest Mother!
   If thou wouldst have us live,
Say that we are thy children,
   And Jesus will forgive.

Our sins make us unworthy
   That title still to bear;
But thou are still our Mother,
   Then show a Mother's care.

Open to us thy mantle;
   There stay we without fear:
What evil can befall us
   If, Mother, thou are near?

O sweetest, dearest Mother!
   Thy sinful children save;
Look down on us with pity
   Who thy protection crave.

APPLICATION. Mary, Queen of heaven and earth, rules the hearts and souls of men. It is often hard to be fair and just in facing all the problems that life presents. Yet, even the most intricate and apparently insurmountable are directed by us to Mary, the Heavenly Queen.

Courtesy of Rev. J. B. Carol, O. F. M.

UNIT SEVEN
RELIGION UNITES CHRISTIAN CIVILIZATION

UNIT SEVEN

RELIGION UNITES CHRISTIAN CIVILIZATION

THE monks and missionaries of the Middle Ages did a truly great work in the days of the barbarian invasions. They copied and preserved manuscripts of ancient times and taught the ways of civilization to the new people in the Empire. However, the greatest achievement of all was the conversion of these new peoples to the Christian religion.

As time went on, a change came over the once pagan empire. Pagan Rome was now Christian Rome. The pagan empire had disappeared. In its place were several nations struggling for power, but rich in the knowledge of the one, true God. By the eleventh century, Christianity reigned supreme throughout the once pagan empire. People often refer to this period of history as the Middle Ages.

The Church also taught the people the right way to get along together. We call this the Church's social teaching. The Church's social teaching guided the people who organized the first towns after the feudal days. Under the patronage of the Church the people grouped together into guilds. These guilds were something like unions are today. The members and officers of these guilds were guided in their duties by the social virtues of justice and charity.

The monastic and cathedral schools of the Middle Ages bore glorious results in the following centuries.

CHAPTER I

RELIGIOUS ORDERS

Looking into the chapter. In Unit Five you learned that the Irish monks and the Benedictines saved civilization during the early Middle Ages. It was not until the thirteenth century that other religious Orders began in the Church. These religious Orders were established by holy men who dedicated their lives to the love and service of God and the salvation of souls.

This chapter tells about the beginnings of these Orders and the work they did in the Church. Each Order had a different purpose and way of life. Yet the spirit of religion which the Orders spread over Europe helped to keep the people united in mind and heart.

1. Dominicans Are Founded

A heresy arises. A strange heresy arose in Europe in the twelfth century. A heresy is a false religious belief which is different from the true teaching of the Church.

The heretics, or those who followed this heresy, were called Albigensians (al-bi-jen'-si-ans). They believed in two gods, one good and one evil. They said it is impossible to lead a good life. This means it is not wrong to lead a bad life. We know this is not right. God expects us all to keep the Commandments if we wish to save our souls and He gives us grace to help us.

This heresy started in France and spread to other countries. It was very dangerous to the souls of the Christians.

At that time, there lived in Spain a very holy man named Dominic. He saw the terrible evil of this heresy and set out to stop it. This was his plan. Saint Dominic set out to preach against this heresy throughout Europe. He explained to them the truths of our holy religion. In doing this he used simple language that the people could understand.

Soon other priests asked if they could join Saint Dominic. This was the beginning of the Dominican Order, also known as the Order of Preachers. Their special work for Christ was the preaching of the Gospel.

The Dominicans are called friars. This word means "brothers." They wore a white habit and a long black cape. They led a regular life of prayer, sacrifice, and preaching under a set of laws, called a Rule.

Saint Dominic sent the friars, two by two, into all the countries of Europe. This is just what Christ had done. He sent His Apostles to preach the Gospel to all nations.

The work of these friars was blessed by God with much success. Today the Dominican priests and Sisters continue to carry on the great work of their holy founder, Saint Dominic.

Our Lady's message. Saint Dominic did not succeed without the help of God. One day Our Lady appeared to Saint Dominic. She told him that she would teach

Brown Brothers

Saint Dominic

him a special way to pray. He was to teach this way of praying to the people. If he taught the people to be faithful to these prayers, Our Lady said that the dreadful heresy would be stopped. Can you guess what these powerful prayers were? They were the prayers of the Rosary, which every Catholic boy and girl today knows so well.

Our Lady told Saint Dominic that the Rosary was pleasing to her. She told him it would bring God's grace upon the world. It would help to convert the people who had fallen into heresy.

The people found out that

Mary was true to her promise. The faith of the people grew stronger. They refused to accept the false teachings. They remained loyal to the Church.

The Rosary still is used by Catholics the world over. Mary still continues to bless and protect those who are faithful to her Rosary. Many Catholic families say the Rosary together each evening. You may be sure that Our Lady will never forsake any member of these faithful families. Does your family pray together?

Brown Brothers
Saint Francis of Assisi

2. Franciscans Are Founded

Saint Dominic was a young boy of twelve in Spain when a boy named Francis was born in Italy, in a town called Assisi. Francis, like Dominic, was chosen by God to give to the world a religious Order of men and women.

The call of Saint Francis. As a young man, Francis loved a gay life. His father was a wealthy merchant of Assisi. However, Francis disliked the life of a merchant and left home to become a soldier.

When Francis returned from war, he was a very different person. He felt that God had a special work for him to do.

Francis began to take care of poor lepers, whom other people avoided. He gave away his money and the goods he owned. He gave all that he had to the poor people.

Francis felt that this kind of a life was pleasing to God. But Francis' life was very displeasing to his father, who pleaded with his son to change his ways.

Lover of poverty. As a result of this disagreement, Francis found himself with no money to spend. His father refused to allow him any more goods or money. He treated Francis as a stranger, and not as a son. Francis did not become sad at this. Many people laughed at him, but still Francis was happy. Do you know why? He was glad to become poor, because of his great love of Christ. This was the reason for Francis' joy and happiness.

Francis wore rich and colorful robes no longer. In their place, he wore a simple grey tunic, or robe, caught around the waist with a piece of rope. He traveled barefoot from place to place. He preached the Gospel and took care of the sick and needy.

Was Saint Francis forced to become poor? No, indeed. He chose to become poor so that he could be more like Christ. Our Lord was poor while He lived on earth, so Francis was poor, too. Money and riches do not make people happy. The happiest people on earth are those who live in the grace of God.

The Poor Man of Assisi. Saint Francis preached to the people in a very simple manner. He treated all men in such a pleasing, kindly way that they felt he was truly their brother. By his kindness he taught people to love God.

Saint Francis loved the animals, the birds, and the bees. Everything God made reminded Saint Francis of the glory of God. He wrote many hymns of praise in his own language, the Italian language.

The Franciscan way of life. Soon many men were asking to join Francis in his work. He welcomed them gladly to the service of God. However, no one could follow Francis unless he became poor. Francis wanted his followers to be poor for Christ's sake.

The Franciscans cared for the sick, helped the peasants in the fields, and taught the Gospel to the poor. These friars did not live in monasteries in the beginning. Instead, they went all over Europe, preaching by word and example.

Saint Francis and the Crib. Saint Francis reminded the people of the true meaning of Christmas. He was the first one to set up a Crib to remind the people of the lowly birth of Christ. In his first Crib, Saint Francis placed figures of the Infant Jesus, Mary, Joseph, and the animals who were in the stable on the night that Christ was born.

Other Franciscan Orders. Shortly afterwards, Saint Francis established a religious order for women. Because Saint Clare was the first Franciscan Sister, the Order became known as the Poor Clares. These Sisters spent much time every day praying that God would bless the work of the Franciscan priests.

Later, Saint Francis formed an Order for lay people; that is, for people living in the world. He made a special Rule for them so that they, too, could share in the good work of the Friars. Do you know any lay people who belong to the Third Order of Saint Francis? Perhaps there are members among your own family and friends.

Do you know some of the special blessings are given to members of the Third Order?

3. Other Followers of Saint Benedict

In an earlier Unit of this text, you learned about the great leader, Saint Benedict and the Order which he founded. Saint Benedict, you know, lived in the sixth century. In the late Middle Ages, three religious Orders arose in the Church. They all took Saint Benedict as their patron and followed his Rule.

Cluny. The first of these new Benedictine Orders was that called the Congregation of Cluny. Cluny is a place in central France. A certain duke of

The monastery at Cluny

Culver Service

France founded a monastery there in 910.

These monks lived very holy lives just as their great patron, Saint Benedict. But the monks of Cluny did not have an abbot as their first superior. They lived directly under the authority of the Pope. This is what made them different from the early Benedictines.

The monks were glad to belong to Cluny. No rich nobles could now interfere with their monastery, since the Pope was in charge of its affairs. About three hundred monasteries were established under the name of the Congregation of Cluny.

Cistercians. Another order which followed the Rule of Saint Benedict was that founded by Saint Robert, at a place called Citeaux (see-toh') in France. The monks came to be called Cistercians (sis-ter'-shens).

The special work of the Cistercians is that of prayer and penance for the sins of the world. Their entire day is spent in silence, work, and spiritual exercises.

A famous monk. When a new Cistercian monastery was to be founded at Clairvaux, a monk named Bernard was made its abbot. This monk did a great work in spreading the houses of his Order. Very often he was called upon by the Pope to perform some special duty. Among the works which he did outside his monastery, perhaps his preaching a Crusade is the most famous. You will learn more about Crusades later.

The strictest Order. Perhaps the strictest Order in the Church is that founded by Saint Bruno. It is called the Carthusian (kar-thoo'-zhen) Order.

The Carthusian Rule is based upon the Benedictine Rule and the practices of the monks of early times. Each monk lives by himself in a place called a cell, or hermitage. He devotes his time during the day to prayer, fasting, penance, and work.

At present there is one house of the Carthusian Order in the United States. There are about 600 Carthusian monks in existence today.

The main work of monks. Monks withdraw from the world to pray. They know that many people do not pray enough. That is why they spend their time in prayer. They pray and offer sacrifices to make up for others who forget God or whose faith is weak.

New Words to Learn

heresy	friar	cell	Clairvaux
manual	poverty	hermitage	Citeaux

Matching Test

Can you match the names in Column A with Column B?

Column A

Saint Dominic
Saint Francis
Saint Bruno
Saint Bernard
Saint Robert

Column B

founder of the Carthusians
a famous Cistercian
preached the Rosary to stop heresy
led a life of holy poverty
one of the founders of the Cistercians

A Memory Test

Answer the following questions:

1. Who first introduced the Crib at Christmas? _____.

2. What Rule is followed by the Cistercians? _____.

3. Who taught Saint Dominic to say the Rosary? _____.

4. What was the name of Saint Bernard's abbey? _____.

5. Who was given full charge of the Congregation of Cluny? _____.

6. What Order of Sisters was founded by Saint Francis? _____.

7. Who was the first Franciscan Sister? _____.

Things to Do

1. Find in your school library a book about Saint Francis and the other saints you read about in this chapter. After you have read the book, discuss the story with your classmates.

2. Since the time Our Lady appeared to Saint Dominic, she has appeared several times and mentioned the Rosary. In 1858 she recited it with Saint Bernadette. Find out to whom she appeared in 1917 and what Our Lady said about the Rosary at that time.

CHAPTER II

CHRISTIAN SOCIAL LIVING IN ACTION

Looking ahead. In the days of feudalism, there were very few towns in Europe. The common people lived on land owned by the lord or noble of the castle. The section in which they lived was called a village. There were many of these villages during the Middle Ages.

As time went on, the common people became more and more independent of their lords. They gradually left the manors and began to live in towns which they founded. These townspeople, as they were called, began to make their living by trade.

In these early days of trade, the people were very united. The guilds to which many of them belonged were under the patronage of the Church.

Christian social living was really carried out in the guilds. Every member aimed to do his work perfectly. Justice and charity were the standards, or

principles, on which the guild members based their conduct.

This chapter tells about the rise of the towns and the work of the guilds in the late Middle Ages.

1. From Farmers to Traders

Increase of trade. So many new articles had been coming into Europe from the Eastern countries that people began to make a living by trade. Even before this, some of the village people worked at trades like shoemaking or carpentry, and they set up shops in which to sell the articles they had made.

Many people set up their shops near a crossroads or bridge. People passing that way would then stop to trade before continuing their journey. Often a town sprang up at these crossroads.

Wherever people began to make a living by trade, there also they came to live. As more and more people settled in one place, a town began to rise in that spot. The increase of trade, then, had much to do with changing the way people lived. Many of them were no longer farmers on the land of the nobles. They became traders in business for themselves. **Townspeople win freedom.** These first towns were really owned by nobles. The people were subject to the lords of their lands. It was the lord who made the laws of the town and appointed the officers.

Very often the nobles were unjust to their townspeople. They would require a toll, or sum of money, from every merchant passing through their land. This was very harmful to the trade of the townspeople. They could not afford to pay these tolls to a number of nobles.

The people desired to make their own laws and elect their own officers in the town. Then they could manage their own affairs without the lords or nobles.

Some towns became wealthy and demanded privileges from

A town in the Middle Ages

the nobles. They gathered an army and fought for their freedom. These towns, of course, were rich in money, men, and goods. Otherwise, the noble would not have to give in to the demands of the people. Do you think it was right for the people to fight for their freedom?

Some townspeople buy freedom. Towards the end of the eleventh century the Crusades began. These were wars to protect the Holy Land. Many nobles wanted to take part in these wars. These nobles owned a great deal of land. But they were poor in money. They could not buy the things they needed for the Crusade.

The townspeople had been trading with others. They had the money which the nobles needed. Very often they gave the nobles the money on condition that they could own the town as their property. In this way, many towns became independent of the nobles.

2. Simple Town Life

Protecting the town. The first towns in Europe were not at all like towns in our country today. Instead, the towns were protected very much like the castles of the feudal days.

High stone walls surrounded the town on every side. These walls were protected by moats, drawbridges, and other means of protection from enemies.

In order to enter a town, during the day, it was necessary to have permission to do so. At a certain time each night, the gates of the town were closed so no one could enter. Would you like to have lived in a town like this?

Very often there was a tower at each side of the large gateway. The tower had narrow windows, so that the townspeople could hurl arrows at any enemy approaching the gate.

No lights, no sidewalks. There were no tall buildings inside the town except the cathedral or church. No one spent any time planning the growth of the town, so the narrow streets would wind in and out in every direction. One could build a house almost any place in town. People did not go out after dark unless it was necessary. There were no street lights, and people would carry a torch to light the way after dark. There were no other services offered by the town, such as a fire department or water system. If a house caught fire, it would be the duty of the owner to do his best to put out the fire. Why are you more fortunate than the people in those old, medieval towns?

Upon a market day. In the days when towns were beginning, there were certain days set apart each week for buying and selling. These days were called market days.

On market day, all the farmers and merchants would bring their carts of goods to the market place. Here they set up stalls where their neighbors could see their *wares,* or goods, which were for sale. These goods would be shoes, clothes, and various articles made by the craftsmen and master workmen of the town.

Come to the fair. Besides the weekly market days, there were fairs held once or twice a year. The fairs lasted usually a week.

When the fair came to town, everybody went to this celebration. Men, women, and even the children were there. It was a time of great gayety and amusement besides business. No one missed the fair when it came to town.

The usual merchants were at their stalls, of course. Besides, there were merchants from distant places, with goods from faraway countries. Some of these articles the people in the town had never seen before. It was a treat for them just to see these strange articles.

Only the rich townspeople could afford to pay the price for such luxuries as pepper and other spices sold by the visiting peddlers. The common people had to do without these goods from distant lands in the East.

In the booths at the fair there were such articles as fine cloth, jewels, and rugs for the homes. Many a person who could not buy these articles knew where they came from. It made them anxious to travel to the East to get these goods for themselves.

Good times at the fair. Today, boys and girls are happy when the circus comes to town. But, in the towns in Europe, the day of the fair was like a circus to the children. Along with the peddlers and merchants came acrobats, musicians, and clowns. The tight-rope walkers, animal trainers, and jugglers were there, too. These people were prepared to amuse the townspeople by putting on a show. Everyone rejoiced to see the fair come to town. Why would you like to have attended a fair?

3. Townspeople at Work

Most of the people lived their religion well. These people put the rules of Christian social living into action. In this section you will see how Christian people practiced charity and justice.

During the Middle Ages, all the men of one trade lived nearby, usually on one street. The goldsmiths had a street for themselves. So did the shoemakers, jewelers, and leathermakers. Every workman used the front windows of his home to display, or show, his goods. These workmen and their families would live in the back of the house or on the second floor.

Life in a shop. One had to know his trade very well before he could own a shop. But in each of these shops there would be some young boys. These boys would learn the trade from the owner of the shop, who was called the master workman.

None of these boys worked for pay while learning the trade. However, he had no need to worry. The master workman fed and clothed him in his own house. He saw to it that the boy kept up the practice and study of his religion while under his charge.

Brown Brothers

A medieval tailor

What would you say of the conduct of the master workman? Do you think he was just? How does this compare with the way a young man begins a trade today?

One who learned a trade in this way was called an apprentice (a-pren′-tis). Most masters treated their apprentices well.

Where does a boy go today to learn a trade? He may go to a special school called trade school, or to a shop where he may learn a trade. But in the Middle Ages, there were no such schools for boys. One learned a trade in the home of a master workman.

The second step to success.
When a boy learned his trade well, he took a strict examination in his trade. If he passed this test, he was called a journeyman.

As a journeyman, the young boy could accept wages for his work. But he could not yet open a shop of his own. He traveled from town to town, working for other master workmen and gaining experience along the way.

The journeyman becomes master.
In order to become a master, the journeyman had to take another examination. For this he had to make his first "masterpiece." A *masterpiece* was the finest article that a man could make in his trade or craft.

It was, indeed, a happy day when a journeyman became a master workman. With this honor came certain privileges. First, he could now open a shop of his own. Second, he could teach others the trade and have apprentices as his own. Third, he would now be allowed to join the guild. The guilds set a just price on products. They saw to it that proper materials were used. They also regulated working conditions. Every trade had its own guild. There was a shoemakers' guild, weavers' guild, tailors' guild, and so on.

4. The Church Guides the Guilds

Each guild was under the protection of a certain saint. On the feast of that saint the members attended Mass together and received Holy Communion. Members of the guild marched in processions on the great feast days of the Church. The religious ideals of the members held them closely together.

Everyone in a guild took pride in his work. The guild members knew that work is dignified. They knew that Christ Himself worked at a trade on earth. Christ sanctified work and gave it His blessing.

Rules of the Guilds. The teachings of the Church called for justice and charity in dealing with other people. Members of the guilds made these rules part of the practice of their daily business life.

Every guild elected its own officers. Dues were charged to pay expenses. The guild officers checked all articles sold so that no one was offered work that was poorly done. These officers punished anyone whose work was found imperfect. There was a punishment also for those who sold goods at too high a price. Masters could be dismissed from the guild for these offenses.

Every workman in the guild charged the same price for goods he sold. This price was decided upon by the officers of the guild. Every workman received the same wages according to the laws of the guild.

If any member became sick or was injured, the guild paid the expenses. The poor of the town were cared for also by the guilds.

Guildhalls. The guild members did not always meet for business meetings. Often they had social gatherings where again the bond of religion united them.

Members of the guilds built beautiful buildings, called guildhalls, where they held banquets and were entertained at certain times.

One popular pastime was the producing of plays. Very often these plays were scenes taken

Guildhalls like these were built in the middle ages. For what were they used?

from the Bible stories. One guild might prepare the story of the creation, and another the flood. Still another might act out the story of the birth of Christ, or the story of the Prodigal Son.

Because some of these stories were about the mysteries of our religion, they came to be called "mystery plays."

Other plays taught important moral lessons for the people to remember. In these one would find a person acting as Pride, another as Anger, or as Kindness. People called these "morality plays."

Learning New Words

wares	journeyman	guilds
fair	crossroads	market day
apprentice	masterpiece	morality plays
toll	miracle plays	

Choosing the correct word

1. A guild was a group of (soldiers, farmers, tradesmen, religious orders).

2. A charge made for passing through a territory was called (toll, fair, masterpiece, apprentice).

3. When a boy became a journeyman, he could receive (honors, wages, masterpieces, apprentices).

4. Sacred scenes played by the guilds were called (operas, dramas, mystery plays, shows).

5. Some towns bought their freedom from (kings, nobles, serfs, the Pope).

6. To learn a trade, a boy first became a(n) (page, serf, apprentice, journeyman).

7. To join a guild, one had to be a(n) (page, master, apprentice, journeyman).

8. If a man charged too high a price for an article, he was punished for being (uncharitable, unjust, lazy, too proud).

9. When a guild took care of poor townspeople, it was practicing (honesty, humility, charity, poverty).

10. Plays that taught a moral lesson were called (mystery plays, Bible plays, stage shows, morality plays).

CHAPTER III

PROGRESS IN CHRISTIAN LEARNING AND CULTURE

A milestone in Christian civilization. The thirteenth century gave the world great religious leaders. These leaders made civilization more Christian and devout. The religious Orders established by these holy men continue to do good.

The guilds of the Middle Ages were established under the patronage of the Church. Members of the guilds placed God's laws first, in the shops, in the market place, and in their own homes. Justice and charity were the keynotes of their lives.

In this chapter we shall study about the very holy and learned teachers of the thirteenth century. The greatest of all teachers was Saint Thomas Aquinas. His writings are of greatest value to the Church in explaining the truths of our holy religion.

The people of the Middle Ages showed their love for God in a very special way. They did everything they could to make the temple of God more beautiful. Every painting, every stained-glass window, was decorated in such a way as to remind the people of holy things. The great love and reverence these people had for God inspired them to build artistic churches and cathedrals.

1. Early Schools

Monks, teachers of the world. During the early days of the Middle Ages the only teachers of Europe were the monks. Because they held their classes in monasteries, their schools were called monastic schools.

When Christianity became more widespread, the bishops of various dioceses began to set up schools near their cathedrals. In the cathedral schools many were given careful instruction in religion and other subjects.

The growth of the towns caused a desire for more learning. In order to carry on a trade one had to know something about arithmetic and the ways of doing business. The people found out that the Arabs in the East had an easier way of counting than they had. It was much easier to write 1,2,3, etc., than the Roman numerals (I, II,III).

The Arabs also taught the people of Europe many other things. Several arts and crafts had first come to Europe through the Arabs.

When the Mohammedans settled in Spain in the time of Charlemagne, they began to teach medicine and science there. They taught the people much about the ancient Greek and Roman civilization.

Learning in the Eastern Empire. You remember that the Eastern Empire did not fall into the hands of barbarians in the fifth century. It survived and continued its ways of civilization. Especially in Constantinople, the best of Greek and Roman writings were preserved and taught.

2. Rise of Universities

Wandering teachers. The students in cathedral schools often had a change of teachers. Many famous teachers did not at first settle in one place. Instead they wandered from place to place giving instructions to eager and willing students. This method had some advantages.

In this way the bishop of a cathedral would invite some great scholar to give lectures, or talks, to the students of his school. This scholar might be an instructor in religion, Latin, science, or medicine. But as soon as soon as his series of lectures was over, he would move on to another city or town where there were other students.

Teachers settle down. As time went on, this manner of teaching died out. Instead, the famous teachers began to settle in one place, such as a growing city or town. Then the students flocked to that place for instruction. Thus, a center of learning arose. This large school became known as a university. The King or the Pope gave a charter or permission for the university to be set up and operate.

Many subjects were taught and many kinds of teachers gathered at a university. Some universities, however, became

Students in a medieval university

famous for special training in certain subjects. The University of Paris became famous for its courses in religion. There were excellent law courses taught at Bologna, Italy, so that university became the center for students of law. At Salerno, Italy, there were famous teachers of medicine. A student anxious to get training to be a doctor would most likely go to that university.

Students controlled some universities. The young students in certain parts of Europe were so eager for learning that they themselves set up universities in their towns. They hired the teachers, gave them a salary, and decided how many hours a day they would teach. The teacher could not have a day off unless the students' gave him permission! One of the universities run by the students was Bologna. Why would you like to have been a student in the days of the late Middle Ages? Would you prefer to study at Paris, where the teachers controlled the university?

Education for all. Universities were open to all classes of people, rich and poor. Some of the students were very poor and led a very hard life during their years of study at the university.

The teacher used no textbook in those days. The professor spoke slowly and the students wrote down carefully what he said. This is how the pupils were taught in the early days of universities.

These students came from all the various countries of Europe and spoke different languages. But these students had learned Latin some time before in monastic or cathedral schools. So the teachers spoke in Latin and the students wrote down the lecture in Latin also. Latin was the language of the university.

The classrooms were very simple. Seats and long benches were set up in any vacant room which the teacher could find.

3. Patron of Schools

One of the greatest Doctors of the Church was born in Italy in the thirteenth century. His name was Saint Thomas Aquinas. Since the time of Saint Augustine, there was no great Christian thinker who would so far surpass his fellow-men in learning. Saint Thomas was to do so.

As a young boy, Saint Thomas entered the Order of Preachers, which we often call the Dominican Order. Like many of the Dominican Fathers of his time, he was sent to a university for further study. It was the custom for many of the religious Orders to build houses of study near the great universities, so that their members could receive the best training possible.

One of Saint Thomas' teachers was Saint Albert the Great, also a Dominican. He was a very learned man. He wrote many books on biology, physics, philosophy, theology and several other subjects. Saint Albert justly deserved to be called "the Great."

Saint Thomas fooled many of his companions in class. He seemed very slow in his studies. Other students called him "The Dumb Ox." But his teacher never believed this. He knew Saint Thomas was a quiet pupil but an excellent student. "One day," said Albert, "this 'ox' will bellow so loud he will be heard throughout the whole world."

Saint Albert the Great was right. His pupil became one of

the most learned men the world has ever known.

Works of Saint Thomas Aquinas. Do you remember Aristotle, the Greek thinker? He was a philosopher, but a pagan one. Still, Aristotle used reason in arriving at his answers to problems of life.

Saint Thomas was a philosopher too. But Saint Thomas was a Christian philosopher. He showed the world that the Christian religion is not against reason. The special subject taught by Saint Thomas is theology. It studies truths about God, and is called "queen of the sciences."

Saint Thomas wrote a famous book on theology, called the *Summa*. When you are older, you will learn more about it.

You most likely have learned some hymns which Saint Thomas wrote. "Adoro Te" and "Tantum Ergo" were written by Saint Thomas. If you own a Missal, look up the Mass for the Feast of Corpus Christi. Saint Thomas composed the prayers and selected the readings from the Bible for that Mass. Because of his great learning, Saint Thomas has been called ''Patron of Schools.''

Brown Brothers
Saint Thomas Aquinas

4. Father of Modern Science

One of the famous teachers of the thirteenth century was a Franciscan friar named Roger Bacon. He also was a student of Albert the Great. Roger taught at Paris and at Oxford University, in England. So great was his learning that he wrote several books for the Pope of that time, on mathematics, religion, and languages.

Roger Bacon was somewhat different from other teachers of his time. He spent a good deal of time trying to find out facts about the world. He tried to find out why certain things happen the way they do.

Experiments begin. Roger Bacon had a workshop, or laboratory, at his monastery in England. Here he worked every day, trying out different experiments. When you are older, you will carry out experiments in science classes.

Many people did not like the way Roger Bacon began to learn new things. Many people did not believe in Roger Bacon's experiments because he was finding out things people never knew before. Roger Bacon even experimented with gunpowder!

Because he was one of the early experimenters, Roger Bacon is called the "Father of Modern Science." Today many wonderful things are being discovered every day by those who are experimenting in science laboratories. Can you name some of these things?

5. Other Great Teachers

Saint Bonaventure. Saint Bonaventure was born in Italy. He joined the Franciscan Order and taught at the University of Paris. He wrote some very important books on theology. He also wrote several books on how to live a good Catholic life. These books are still read and followed today.

Saint Bonaventure became a Cardinal as well as the head of the whole Franciscan Order. His feast day is celebrated on July 14.

John Scotus. Another great Franciscan teacher was John Scotus. He was born in England. After becoming a Franciscan he taught theology at Oxford and Paris. He also wrote very important books on theology.

John Scotus is famous for his love for the Blessed Mother. He played a very important part in helping to explain the Church's teaching on Mary's Immaculate Conception.

Great hymns. Can you sing the first verse of the "Stabat Mater"? That beautiful hymn was written in the thirteenth century. It is still sung in our churches during Lent and especially during the Stations of the Cross.

At funerals and some other Requiem Masses, there is a beautiful hymn, called the "Dies Irae," recited by the priest. It is written in Latin, just as the "Stabat Mater," and it rhymes in Latin, just as poetry often does in the English language. Perhaps you have already learned the first verse of the "Dies Irae." If so, you can sing a hymn that is over seven hundred years old! Only very beautiful and worthwhile songs last as long as that. Few songs are that old.

The greatest poet. In Florence, Italy, there lived a man called Dante. He, too, began to write poetry, but not in Latin. He used the Italian language as he heard it spoken in Tuscany, the section of Italy where he lived.

Dante wrote a very long poem called "The Divine Comedy." It is about the life hereafter. It describes Hell, Purgatory, and Heaven as Dante imagined them to be. This work of Dante makes him one of the greatest poets of the world.

A medieval cathedral

Screen Traveler from Gendreau

Brown Brothers

Saint Patrick's Cathedral

6. The Pride of Every Town

You have seen how some towns became famous. Some of them possessed within their walls a famous university, which attracted students from all parts of the world.

There was something else, however, which made some towns famous. That was a cathedral, or large church. The people expressed their great love and reverence for God by making their cathedrals very beautiful.

The guilds had much to do with the building of the cathedrals. All the members were anxious to contribute their best work to the building of God's House.

Churches of former days. The first churches in the Roman Empire were just like other Roman buildings. When the monks built their monasteries and churches, they made their roofs of stone. That is why there were heavy columns or pillars inside the monastery. The walls, too, had to be very solid. That is why there were no large windows in them. As a result, the monasteries and churches were often dark.

Change in architecture. When the towns began building churches, they changed the style of the building. This change was in the way the roof was supported.

There were stone supports built outside the church to strengthen the roof. These were called *buttresses*. Inside, ribbed vaults in the ceiling helped to do this, too.

Now that the stone roof was better supported, much larger windows could be put in the side walls. These windows were decorated with stained-glass pictures of Our Lord, Our Lady, and the saints. Sometimes the windows described some scene in the life of Our Lord, or a story told by Him.

Sculptors kept themselves busy preparing statues for their cathedral. They wanted to remind the people of the sacredness of the church.

Often the cathedrals had graceful, stately spires that seemed to point up to heaven like an act of faith in God. This kind of architecture is called Gothic.

The Cathedral of Notre Dame in Paris and Saint Patrick's Cathedral in New York are examples of Gothic architecture.

Who built the cathedrals. We do not know much about the architects of the great cathedrals. We know that some of them were monks.

The actual stone-cutting, carving, and building were done by people of the neighborhood. People who could not carve statues or do other skilled work helped to quarry the stones or hauled them to the building.

Anyone who worked on the cathedral was supposed to go to Confession and Holy Communion first. At night, after work was over, the people gathered to pray and sing hymns. Building a cathedral was a work done in honor of God and Our Lady.

Can you see now why the cathedrals have been called "prayers in stone"?

New Words for Your Study

university	experimenting
lecture	laboratory
Summa	buttress
theology	vault

Things to Discuss and Do

Answer the following questions about Saint Thomas.

1. Give the year and country in which he was born.
2. Name his most important work.
3. In what place was Saint Augustine bishop?
4. With what university was Saint Thomas connected?
5. Why is Saint Thomas called the Patron of Schools?

Completion Test

1. The University of Bologna was noted for the study of ——————.

2. —————— is the study of truths related to God.

3. The Summa was written by Saint ——————.

4. A learned Dominican who taught Saint Thomas was Saint ——————.

5. Schools which taught many subjects for older students were called ——————.

6. Language of the lecturer at these schools was always ——————.

7. If a boy wanted to study medicine, he would perhaps go to ——————.

8. The chief study associated with the University of Paris was ——————.

9. Cathedrals of the late Middle Ages were usually built with —————— to support the walls.

10. In the Middle Ages, people placed in their churches —————— windows, illustrating a Bible story or the life of some saint.

Review of Unit Seven

Reread this Unit. Then write on your paper three of the most important facts connected with the following:

1. Famous religious Orders which arose during the late Middle Ages.
2. The rise of towns and the kind of workers employed in the guilds.
3. Famous teachers at universities of the thirteenth century.

Mastery Test for Unit Seven

I. Answer the following questions briefly.

1. Who founded the religious Order known as Order of Preachers?
2. What special devotion was given to the world to fight heresy?
3. Who was called the "Poor Man of Assisi"?
4. What is the name of the religious Order to which Saint Bernard belonged?
5. What is the sum of money paid for passing through a person's property?
6. The people of the same trade belonged to what organization similar to a union today?
7. A work of special perfection was called by what term?
8. In the guildhalls, what kind of plays often took place?
9. What was the name of the tower which protected the town from enemies?
10. What building was constructed to show the people's great faith and love of God?

II. Place the following in the order of their occurrence.

schools in the Roman Empire
cathedral schools

monastic schools
universities

III. Place the following in the correct order.

journeyman
apprentice

master workman

IV. Matching Test.

On your paper, write full sentences about each name in Column A by using the correct phrase in Column B.

Column A	Column B
1. Saint Albert the Great	...... studied by means of experimenting
2. Roger Bacon	...... belonged to the Dominicans; wrote the Summa
3. Saint Clare	...... preached a Crusade
4. Saint Bernard	...... was a learned Dominican who taught at Cologne
5. Saint Thomas Aquinas	...... asked Saint Francis to write a rule for women
6. Saint Robert	...... helped to found a monastery at Citeaux
7. Saint Francis	...... founded the Franciscans

V. Answer "Yes" or "No" to the following questions on your paper.

1. Did the teachers at the universities speak to the students in Latin?
2. Were the guilds under the patronage of the Church?
3. Did the Arabs teach Roman numerals to the people of Europe?
4. Did Saint Francis preach in Latin?
5. Did every student at the university study the same subjects?
6. Was Oxford a famous university in Italy?
7. Is Albert the Great called "Patron of the Schools"?
8. Were the Franciscans called the Order of Preachers?
9. Did Dante write in Italian?
10. Was Albert the Great a German?
11. Could one buy goods from distant places at the town fair?
12. Were the miracle plays put on by members of the guilds?
13. Was Roger Bacon interested in science?
14. Did Saint Thomas Aquinas write the Mass for Corpus Christi?
15. Did an apprentice earn wages for his work?
16. Did Pope Innocent III approve of the Franciscan and Dominican Orders?

VI. Answer the following in complete sentences.

1. Why were the guild members somewhat like union members today?
2. What was the purpose of the guild?
3. Why is theology called the queen of sciences?

Hymns to Mary

HISTORY OF HYMNS. A little over a hundred years ago a number of gifted men in England, became converts. They were interested in the history of Christianity, and many wrote and translated the early hymns. Cardinal Newman was the outstanding convert in this group, and he was one of the first to make translations of the Latin hymns. Another famous translator of Latin hymns was Father Edward Caswall who translated some of the hymns from the Breviary.

ORIGIN AND MEANING. The hymn, "O Most Holy One" is a translation of the hymn to the Blessed Virgin, "O Sanctissima." It was translated by an American convert, Father J. M. Raker, who died in 1947. After his conversion and ordination, Father Raker served in the diocese of La Crosse, Wisconsin. Always interested in improving hymn-writing, he published a hymnal.

"O Most Holy One"

O most holy one,
O most lowly one,
　　Dearest Virgin *Maria!*
Mother of fair Love,
Home of the Spirit Dove,
　　Ora, ora pro nobis.

Help in sadness drear,
Port of gladness dear,
　　Virgin Mother *Maria!*
In pity heeding,
Hear thou our pleading
　　Ora, ora pro nobis.

Call we fearfully,
Sadly, tearfully
　　Save us now, *O Maria!*
Let us not languish,
Heal thou our anguish,
　　Ora, ora pro nobis.

Mother, Maiden fair,
Look with loving care,
　　Hear our prayer, *O Maria!*
Our sorrow feeling,
Send us thy healing,
　　Ora, ora pro nobis.

APPLICATION. Mary, the refuge of sinners, accepted God's plan for her.
In sin and in evil, we look for help, seeking refuge in safe surroundings, and anxious to cleanse our souls spiritually.

Courtesy of Rev. J. B. Carol, O. F. M.

UNIT EIGHT

A NEW WORLD AWAITS CHRISTIAN CIVILIZATION

UNIT EIGHT

A NEW WORLD AWAITS CHRISTIAN CIVILIZATION

About 1300, some people in Italy began to take a new interest in the art and writings of ancient Rome and Greece.

Writers, such as Petrarch, began to glorify certain ancient pagan ideas of learning and civilization. Painters, sculptors, and inventors throughout Europe joined the list of those seeking this "new birth" in learning. This period is called the "Renaissance" (ren'-a-sahns).

It was during this Renaissance Period that the age of discovery and invention began. But the steps towards the discovery of America really began in the days of the Crusades.

It was during the Crusades that the West first saw and heard about the wonderful riches of the Eastern countries. The merchants of Europe went to the East for these goods. All went well until Constantinople fell. Land routes were closed.

The desire for a water route to India led several countries to explore for one. While Spain was searching for such a route, one of her explorers found a great new world. That world is your country, America, Land of Our Lady!

This last Unit of *Founders of Freedom* tells you about some events that led up to the discovery of America. The story of the discoverers of America and the nations who made colonies there is told in BEARERS OF FREEDOM, the next book of this series.

CHAPTER I

STRIFE IN EUROPE AND THE EAST

The Crusades and the Hundred Years' War. You have been studying about the Christian spirit that united the Christian world in the thirteenth century.

This spirit did not extend to lands in the East, however. There was a great struggle going on in the Holy Land, the land where Christ lived on earth.

The Christians of Europe did a great work in trying to free the Holy Land from the Turks. The many wars fought did not always end in victory. However, many other good things resulted from these Crusades. We shall see what they were.

The nations of Europe had become strong enough to carry on war for many years. England and France were the warring nations. This war would have turned out differently if God had not raised up a leader for the French.

1. Crusades—Wars of the Cross

Freedom's road leads to the Holy Land. Have you ever heard about a pilgrimage? A pilgrimage is a journey to a holy place. Some of the greatest pilgrimages of all times led to places in the Holy Land. Even today many go there.

These places were made sacred by the birth, life, and death of our Lord. The people of the Middle Ages loved to visit these holy places. For hundreds of years they went to Jerusalem and the Holy Land. The Arabs, who were Mohammedans, had taken possession of the sacred places. Yet, they still allowed the Christians to visit there, provided they paid a tax.

The Turks capture Jerusalem. About 1071 a fierce tribe of Mohammedan Turks conquered the Arabs. They refused to allow any more pilgrims to come to the holy places. When the

Philip Gendreau, N. Y.

The Crusaders fought for holy places around Jerusalem

Christians kept coming these Turks killed hundreds of them.

Soon dreadful stories of the sufferings of the pilgrims were told in western Europe. It looked as if Christianity in the East would be destroyed.

The call for aid. The Greek Emperor at Constantinople feared the Turks and tried to defeat them in battle, but they were too powerful for his army. This emperor was a Christian but he had some time before separated his empire from the rule of the Pope. He did this because he wanted to control the Church as well as the empire. We know what an evil desire this was for the Greek Emperor of Constantinople.

Now, however, his empire was in great danger. The Turks were conquering his land. He asked the Pope for help in driving the Turks away. The Pope heeded the Emperor's request. But he did so because he wanted to save the holy places rather than merely to help the Emperor.

The Pope preaches a Crusade. Pope Urban called a meeting at Clermont, in France. A great crowd of bishops, nobles, and common people was present there. The Pope told them about the sufferings of the pilgrims. He begged the knights and nobles to stop fighting among themselves. He asked them to raise an army and win back the holy tomb of Christ from the Turks. "Christ Himself," he cried, "will be your Leader when you fight for Jerusalem! Let your quarrels cease, and turn your arms against the Turks."

The people became very excited when they heard the Pope's words. Knights and nobles drew their swords and waved their banners. All cried with one voice, "God wills it!" The Pope then said that "God wills it" should be the battle cry.

Pope Urban reminded them of Our Lord's own words, "If anyone will come after Me, let him take up his cross and follow Me." Thinking of this, they placed crosses of red cloth on their cloaks and painted crosses on their shields. Thus all men might know that they were going on a Crusade or a "war of the Cross."

The First Crusade. The first Crusade was known as the Knights' Crusade. It was led by lords

Brown Brothers
Crusaders in battle

and nobles in 1097 and was successful. After driving the Turks out of Jerusalem, a Christian kingdom was set up in Palestine. Once again the pilgrims could come and go in peace, visiting the holy places.

2. Failure of the Crusades

From time to time the Turks made war on this Christian kingdom. Then other great armies of Crusaders came from Europe to fight the enemy. Rich and poor, young and old, joined their forces to drive the Turk away from the holy places. The greatest number of Crusaders, however, were the common people.

Children's Crusade. Even the children became so excited about the Crusades they decided to go on one of their own. They did not ask the Pope for permission but started out under the leadership of a boy. There was so much excitement that no one stopped them. However, they did not reach the Holy Land. Some were lost or died on the way; others were kidnapped and sold as slaves in Africa. This Crusade is known as the Children's Crusade.

Crusaders lose. All together, there were eight Crusades fought. They were led by knights, nobles, and sometimes kings. The great Saint Bernard, the Cistercian, preached throughout Europe, urging people to join the Second Crusade. Although he was a monk, he did this at the command of the Pope. The third Crusade was called the Kings' Crusade.

Occasionally, the Crusades were successful. Many of them were not. Sometimes the Crusaders did not even get near Palestine. Some were captured, and others died before they reached there.

The power of the Turks was so great that, in 1291 they won back the control of the Holy Land. Thus the Crusades failed

Brown Brothers

A Crusader

in their chief purpose. However, they succeeded in keeping the Turks from attacking all Europe.

Some Crusaders were bad. It would not be correct to think that all the Crusaders went to the East for holy, pious reasons. Many rich nobles went to gain more riches, while others went just for the love of adventure. These people did more harm than good. Some were guilty of robberies and even the murder of innocent people in Palestine. They displeased God by their actions, instead of giving greater glory to God. This was not God's will for the Crusaders.

3. The Maid of Orleans

When the Crusades were over, most of Europe was at peace. However, there were two nations in Europe constantly at war. These were England and France. Each one sought greater power and wealth for itself.

England had claim to some land in France. This annoyed the French king and nobles. The slightest reason was enough to start a war.

England and France went to war in 1346. They finished this war in 1453. They were fighting off and on, for about one hundred years, so it became known as the Hundred Years' War. Most of the time the French were the losers.

Many died of sickness. While thousands lost their lives on the battlefield, other thousands of people died all over Europe of a dreadful disease known as the "Black Death." It caused the sick person severe agony which usually ended in death.

Farming and manufacturing were almost at a standstill for a few years. The Church lost many of its priests who caught the disease as they gave the dying the last Sacraments.

In England the disease was especially bad, and very few priests escaped. Since the people were left with very few priests, it was hard to go to Mass and receive the Sacraments. You know that without these helps, faith grows weak.

After the nations recovered from the Black Death, the Hundred Years' War continued. The English attacked the city of Orleans in France. France was almost completely beaten. All true French people were very sad to see this happen to their country.

Voices from Heaven. At this time in France there lived a poor peasant girl named Joan. She began to hear beautiful voices calling to her while she was at prayer. These voices told her to go save France.

This seemed impossible to Joan. She did not even know how to ride a horse, much less lead an army into battle.

For three years the voices kept calling to Joan. They kept repeating that it was God who was commanding her to save France. At last she determined to go to see the Dauphin (daw'-fin). The Dauphin was the eldest son of the last king, and the throne of France rightfully belonged to him.

At first the Dauphin refused to see this young warrior girl.

Saint Joan of Arc
Brown Brothers

present at the coronation of Charles VII in the beautiful cathedral at Rheims.

A sad event happened to Joan soon afterwards. Some of the French generals were jealous of her success. Instead of rewarding her for her heroic work, they allowed the English to capture her. They made her suffer in prison for more than a year.

Then, after an unjust trial, Joan was condemned to death by the English. She was condemned to be burned at the stake. This unjust sentence was carried out on May 30, 1431. It was a day many would remember with great sorrow.

But at last she got to see him. She said she would save France and see the Dauphin crowned King at Rheims, where other French kings had been crowned.

The Dauphin at last gave Joan a beautiful white horse, a suit of shining armor, and an army of men to lead to Orleans. She proudly bore the banner of France to the battlefield.

Savior of France. After a terrible battle at Orleans, the English were defeated and France was saved. Joan of Arc is often called Savior of France or the Maid of Orleans. She had the happiness of being

Saint Joan's Prison
Screen Traveler from Gendreau

279

As the flames reached up to burn her in death she called only for Jesus to help her. In 1920, Joan of Arc, the Maid of Orleans, became Saint Joan of Arc. Her feast falls on May 30.

Using Our New Words

Can you use these words in sentences?

pilgrims
Holy Land
Black Death

Crusade
Hundred Years' War
Maid of Orleans

Using Our New Words

1. Why were the Crusades called "Wars of the Cross"?
2. For what reasons did people join the Crusades?
3. Why did the English burn to death the Maid of Orleans?
4. How did it happen that a monk named Saint Bernard preached a Crusade?
5. Why were the wars between England and France called the "Hundred Years' War"?

Yes-No Test

1. Were the Christians allowed to visit the Holy Land before 1071?
2. Did the Greek Emperor fear an attack from the Turks?
3. Did Pope Urban come to the help of the Greek Emperor?
4. Did the people make "God wills it!" the battle cry of the Crusades?
5. Was the freeing of the Holy Land the only aim of all the Crusaders?
6. Was Jerusalem held by the Christians at the end of the First Crusade?
7. Did children attempt to go on a Crusade to free the tomb of Our Lord from the Turks?
8. Was Charles VII called the Dauphin before he was crowned?
9. Did Joan of Arc save France from the Turks?
10. Did the French drive the English out of France?

CHAPTER II

STEPS TO A NEW WORLD

Europe at the crossroads. So far in your study of history you have been traveling over Europe and the East. You have discovered many founders of freedom in your travels, but these founders lived many years ago in Europe.

Now you are about to study the events that took place in Europe just before your own land, America, was discovered. These events are important for you to know. If some of these had not taken place, perhaps America would not have been discovered in 1492 at all.

Many events were happening in Europe during this period. Feudalism had disappeared. People developed a desire for learning which they thought was very different from the thirteenth century learning. Painters, sculptors, writers, and scientists took part in this so-called "new birth." A new spirit was in the air.

The scientists helped greatly to hasten the age of discovery. They invented many things which helped sailors greatly at sea.

We shall read about some of the other events in Europe which led to the discovery of America, the Land of Our Lady.

1. Return of Old Ideas

The Church continues to influence the world. In Italy in the fourteenth century there were many students who had come from Constantinople. These students brought with them Greek ideas about learning and art.

Now the people of Italy had always spoken Latin in their university classes. They knew much about ancient learning of Rome. From the Eastern students they learned much more about the Greek civilization. There arose a great desire for even more learning of this kind. Manuscripts of the past were needed badly.

The Pope helps. In this search for learning of the past, Pope Nicholas V was one of the leaders. He sent messengers in search of these manuscripts to all leading countries of Europe. In this way the great Vatican Library was started in Rome.

Great painters. It was during this period that Michelangelo, a great painter, as well as poet, sculptor and architect, did his greatest work in Rome. He painted scenes from the Bible on the ceiling and walls of the Sistine (sis'-teen) Chapel. The Sistine Chapel is the Pope's chapel in the Vatican Palace.

A very famous painter of this period also worked at the Vatican. His name was Raphael and he painted, among others, the famous "Sistine Madonna." A Madonna is a painting of Our Blessed Mother and the Child Jesus. Many painters gave the world their ideas of the Madonna by their paintings during this period.

"The Last Supper" by Da Vinci is another of the greatest paintings. Leonardo Da Vinci could do many other things besides paint. He was an inventor,

Brown Brothers

The Sistine Chapel

a writer, an engineer, and a musician.

Great sculptors and writers. Michelangelo was the sculptor of a very beautiful figure of Christ in His Mother's arms at the foot of the cross. This piece of sculpture is called the Pieta (pee-a-tah').

There were other sculptors also who began to develop their talent for this art. But they did not select sacred subjects for their work. Instead, they read about ancient Greek heroes and made statues of them. Their idea was to get away from Christian subjects and imitate the pagan artists.

Some of the writers also

broke away from writing about Christian subjects. They imitated the old Latin and Greek poets. They wrote about the gods and goddesses. Soon, some of these writers even began to think like pagans. Some of them no longer believed all the teachings of the Church.

Learning in general. This new idea of learning spread all over Europe during the fourteenth to seventeenth centuries. It emphasized pagan learning of the past, and called it "a new birth" of learning, or Renaissance. Renaissance is a French word and means "rebirth."

Some of the artists and writers of the Renaissance were good men. They followed the Church's teachings even though they studied old Greek and Latin ideas. These men knew that the Church respected everything that was good about ancient learning. The Church taught such ancient learning in the universities.

However, some of the leaders of the Renaissance forgot their debt to the Church.

Changes in architecture. Churches and cathedrals which were built during the Renaissance did not have the buttress and vaults of the thirteenth-century cathedrals. The Renaissance builders did not like this Gothic style. Instead they modeled their structures on those of the ancient Greeks and Romans.

You will recall that the Greeks used columns to support the roofs of their buildings and the Romans used the arch in their structures. The new buildings of the Renaissance did the same.

Saint Peter's in Rome was built during this era. Do you know that many of our public buildings are built in the Greek and Roman style? Perhaps your state capitol or local court house is one of these.

2. Inventions, a Step to Discovery

The Renaissance Period gave the world many new inventions also. These inventions helped to make it easy for the explorers later on.

Printing. Before printing was invented, everything important had to be copied by hand. Anything that people wanted to read was copied down in longhand letter by letter. This was a long and wearisome task.

A German named Gutenberg changed all this. He invented movable type and a printing press. This press was very sim-

Brown Brothers
Saint Peter's Church, Rome

ple compared with the printing presses of today. Yet it had a set of type letters which he arranged to fit a printed page. The first things Gutenberg printed were a large missal and the Latin version of the Bible. If you ever visit Washington, you may see a copy of this Bible at the Library of Congress. It was printed in 1454. Other copies of this Bible are in various parts of the world.

Two hundred years before this, a book had been written out in longhand. People waited their turns to read it. It was called, "Marco Polo's Travels." Gutenberg also printed this story because everyone wanted

to read it. It told of the rich lands in the Orient.

The compass. The Chinese had first invented the compass, which tells direction. But it was not until this period of history that it became useful to the sailors. With a compass, the sailors could always tell if they were going in the right direction. You can understand that this invention helped greatly to encourage journeys by sea.

The astrolabe. The astrolabe was used to sight the stars. By means of this instrument and certain charts sailors could tell at what place their ship might be.

3. Europe Wants a Route to the East

The Crusades changed the Old World. Although the Crusades failed as a whole, they had other important results. They changed the Old World's ways of living.

First, the knights and nobles came back to Europe and found a change in power. The kings now had become strong. Feudalism had been broken by the rise of towns.

Second, the Crusaders saw and used many strange and wonderful things when they were in the East. They saw silks, precious gems, carpets, spices, and rich foods. They liked these things very much, and wanted more of them.

Many former Crusaders returned to the East for some of these wonderful articles. They began to carry on a trade with the East. Merchants made long and dangerous journeys to obtain these goods for their customers.

Routes are closed. This was all very well. But something happened that made them very sad. The Turks had conquered Constantinople in 1453. Now it would be still more dangerous to travel that way to the East.

Since there was no way by land, perhaps a water route could be found. Europe wanted a route to the East.

4. America, Land of Our Lady

Many explorers set out on this difficult task. Someone believed that the earth was round and he could reach the East by sailing West. That man was Christopher Columbus.

Columbus was right about this. But he did not find the lands of the East. Instead, he found a great new world that lay between Europe and the Orient. This world is the con-

A caravel

tinent on which you live— America. The year of this great discovery is 1492, a date we should all remember.

The Old World meets the New World. In the beginning of this text you were told why you are studying about the Old World this year. You learned that the freedom we have in America began in the Old World. You have passed through the centuries from the creation of the world until that October day in 1492 when a new world was discovered.

Those heroes you have been reading about were the FOUNDERS OF FREEDOM. As soon as the new world was discovered, people from the Old World came to the New. Fortunately for us, they brought to the New World the freedom they enjoyed in the Old. You can read about these heroes in BEARERS OF FREEDOM.

Learning New Words

Renaissance
Pieta
Sistine Chapel
Vatican

compass
astrolabe
Madonna

Thing to Do

1. Find in your library as many pictures of the Madonna as you can. List on a paper some of the authors and painters who lived during the Renaissance.

2. Inquire as to what type of building your state capitol is; your church; your local court house.

3. Find pictures in other magazines of famous paintings and sculptures of the Renaissance period.

4. Prepare a report on one of the painters or writers of the period. Make it no more than four sentences but tell some famous work of the person chosen.

Matching

Column A	Column B
1. Nicholas V	...... printing press and type
2. Da Vinci	...... Pieta
3. Michelangelo	...... Sistine Madonna
4. Raphael	...... Last Supper
5. Gutenberg	...... Vatican Library

Review of Unit Eight

1. Crusades, or Wars of the Cross, were carried on because the Holy Land was in danger of being destroyed by the Turks.

2. The First Crusade (1096) was successful.

3. During the Hundred Years'
War, a young girl named Joan of Arc led the French to victory.

4. Joan of Arc had the Dauphin crowned king of France at Rheims.

5. Joan of Arc was betrayed into the hands of the English

and put to death.

6. The people of Italy began to emphasize more fully the ancient learning in the fourteenth century. This was the beginning of the Renaissance Period, which means "new birth."

7. Pope Nicholas V gathered ancient manuscripts and commenced the Vatican Library.

8. Michelangelo and Raphael were famous painters during the Renaissance Period.

9. Gutenberg invented movable types and the printing press about 1454. Other inventions that helped toward the age of discovery were the compass and astrolabe.

10. The victory of the Turks at Constantinople in 1453 led to the desire for a water route to the East.

11. America, Land of Our Lady, was discovered in 1492.

Mastery Test for Unit Eight

I. Answer these questions on your paper.

1. Who was the Maid of Orleans? _____

2. Who invented the printing press? _____

3. What word means "new birth"? _____

4. What were the Wars of the Cross called? _____

5. What city was captured by Turks in 1453? _____

6. What Crusade did Saint Bernard preach? _____

7. What country was defeated in the Hundred Years' War? _____

8. Who sculptured the Pieta? _____

9. Who discovered America? _____

10. Who saved France from the enemy? _____

II. Matching Test

Column A	Column B
1. pilgrims	...... used the compass to tell direction
2. Crusaders	...... were in control of Holy Land
3. Turks	...... visited holy places to pray
4. sailors	...... fought to save the Holy Land
5. painters and sculptors	...... were part of the Renaissance movement

III. Complete the following sentences.

1. The first Crusade was preached by Pope _____.
2. The Crusades were fought in the country of _____.
3. The motto of the Crusaders was: "_____."
4. The first Crusade was known as the _____ Crusades.
5. During the Hundred Years' War, many people died of the _____.
6. Joan of Arc was victorious at the Battle of _____.
7. After the Bible, the first book printed was "_____."
8. During the Renaissance, architecture changed to the old _____ style.
9. The Crusades made the people of Europe desire _____ of the East.
10. Instead of a route to the East, Columbus discovered a _____.

IV. Write "Yes" or "No" after these statements on your paper.

1. The Crusades helped feudalism to die out in Europe.
2. The Pope advised the children to go on a Crusade.
3. Pope Urban II built the Vatican Library.
4. A pilgrimage is a journey to a holy place.
5. All the Crusades were successful.
6. Joan of Arc obeyed the command of the voices from heaven.
7. Pagan heroes and Greek scholars were sculptured during the Renaissance.
8. The Turks were conquered at Constantinople in 1453.
9. Gutenberg invented the compass.
10. The desire for a water route led to the discovery of America.

V. Place these in the right historical order.

...... Saint Thomas Aquinas taught at Paris in thirteenth century.

...... The Renaissance took place in Italy.

...... Charlemagne was crowned Holy Roman Emperor.

...... Columbus discovered America.

Do the same with these.

...... Christ redeemed the world by His death.

...... Moses received the Ten Commandments.

...... Saint Francis founded his religious Order.

...... You are living in the New World.

INDEX